Table of Contents

1390142

The Ex-Offender's Guide to a
Responsible Life

A National Directory of
Re-Entry Tips and Resources

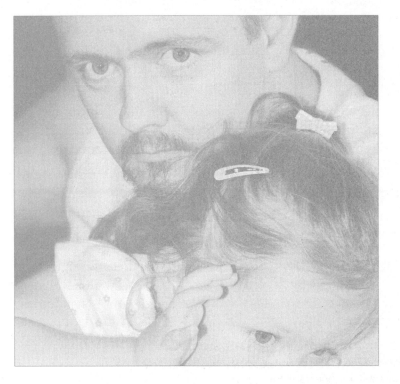

Dr. Harvey E. Shrum, Ed.D.

Impact Publications
Manassas Park, VA

ISBN: 978-1-57023-327-2 (13-digit); 1-57023-327-6 (10-digit)

Library of Congress: 2011944806

Publisher: For information on Impact Publications, including current and forthcoming publications, authors, press kits, online bookstore, and submission requirements, visit the left navigation bar on the front page of the publisher's main company website: www.impactpublications.com.

Publicity/Rights: For information on publicity, author interviews, and subsidiary rights, contact the Media Relations Department: Tel. 703-361-7300, Fax 703-335-9486, or email: query@impactpublications.com.

Sales/Distribution: All bookstore sales are handled through Impact's trade distributor: National Book Network, 15200 NBN Way, Blue Ridge Summit, PA 17214, Tel. 1-800-462-6420. All special sales and distribution inquiries should be directed to the publisher: Sales Department, IMPACT PUBLICATIONS, 9104 Manassas Drive, Suite N, Manassas Park, VA 20111-5211, Tel. 703-361-7300, Fax 703-335-9486, or email: query@impactpublications.com.

Introduction

EX-OFFENDERS NEED useful re-entry tools that help them survive, re-adjust, and stay out for good. Going beyond mere survival, this book offers life-long tools for a meaningful and responsible life. If used properly, the tools outlined here will help you achieve your dreams of being truly free, happy, and productive.

Our Needs, Our Lives

We all have needs – to live and survive, to love and be loved, to feel important, and to have variety. When these needs go unmet, we often resort to addictive and aggressive behaviors to fill the void. But even when all of these needs have been satisfied, we often end up feeling depressed. Needs and wants are not enough. Indeed, human beings also need meaning and purpose in their lives.

Meaning and Purpose

What really motivates you? Some noted psychotherapists, such as Sigmund Freud, believe that human behavior is driven by the **desire for pleasure**. Others, such as Alfred Adler, claim that human behavior is driven by the **desire for power and feelings of superiority**. And still others, such as Viktor Frankl, feel it is a by-product of **doing something meaningful**.

Meaning, noted Viktor Frankl (*Man's Search for Meaning*), **is the ultimate goal**. When we lack meaning, we feel emptiness. The temptation is to vicariously fill that void with pleasure, power, or prosperity. Meaning cannot be taught. It cannot be given. It must be lived by doing and discovering. Often, it requires that we be **patient**. After all, meaning is not always readily known, sometimes not for years. Then we suddenly discover that all suffering are actually **gifts**, ones that nobody wants!

Meaning, emphasized Frankl, **is discovered experientially, creatively, and attitudinally**. **Experientially** we achieve meaning through unique experiences, encounters with others, and in loving relationships. Sometimes life experiences "break" us. But we can become stronger in the broken places of our lives, just as a mended bone tends to be the strongest part of a bone. Drugs, alcohol, or anger and aggression only delay the mending – the transformation.

Creatively we achieve meaning through **creative works and deeds**. Creative works may involve mechanically working on our car, decorating our home, creating a song, a poem, a short story, or other hobbies and leisure activities. It generally involves something that **we enjoy doing** and gives our life meaning. Parenting and relationships can be creative endeavors. As a parent, choosing to be present in our children's lives 24/7 makes our life meaningful. Deeds on the other hand may involve giving back to our community a part of ourselves in the form of volunteer work.

Attitudinally we achieve meaning in the attitude we take toward unavoidable suffering or fate. Death, guilt, and suffering are life events that are inescapable. It is not so much what happens to us that counts however, but the attitudes we take toward what happens to us. It is useless to ask why things happened to us; the useful approach is to **ask what we can do in the situation in which we find ourselves,** be it the death of a loved one, or growing up in the home of a physically or emotionally absent father, or surviving physical, emotional, or sexual abuse.

Meaning must be lived by doing and discovering. It may take years to discover it.

In the absence of an advocate, we may have self-medicated or diverted our anger toward others. It often results in broken relationships, underemployment, traumatic illnesses, or other hardships. Inescapable pain and suffering are gifts that nobody wants or wishes upon others.

Discover the Meaning of Your Life!

During the transition from incarceration to a responsible future, life asks, "What now?" Like a mentor or good friend, the following pages will assist you in discovering the meaning of your life.

If you want to discover the meaning of your life – your purpose – I recommend reading Frankl's *Man's Search for Meaning*, Joseph Fabry's *Guideposts to Meaning*, or my book, *Search for Meaning at the Broken Places*. "You are human beings," Viktor Frankl told the men incarcerated at San Quentin State Prison, "like me, and as such you were free to commit a crime, to become guilty. Now, however, you are responsible for overcoming guilt by rising above it, by growing beyond yourselves, by changing for the better," by turning a predicament or tragedy into a unique achievement or triumph!

May your life be **meaningful!**

Chapter I

Community Resources for Re-Entering Society

*"Get all the advice you can and you will succeed;
without it you will fail."*

Request Information in Writing

If time is not an issue, write to agencies or organizations to request information using the format below. Otherwise, go to your institution or local public library and search on the Internet. Library personnel can assist you if you need help on the computer.

(Name of contact person)
(Today's date)
(Name of agency/organization)
(Street address or P.O. Box #)
(City, State, Zip Code)

Sirs: (or name of contact person)

I am (your name). I plan to settle/return to (city/area) soon. I am looking for assistance in obtaining (state need: food, clothing, housing, employment, counseling, etc.). If you or your organization is unable to assist me, I would greatly appreciate a referral to someone who can assist me. I am looking forward to a meaningful and responsible future and to giving back to my community with its help.

Thank you for your time and assistance with this request.

Sincerely,

(Your signature)
(Typed/Printed name)
(Address)

Federal, State, County, and City Resources

Federal, state, county, and city listings of useful community re-entry resources can be found in the front of a telephone book. Here's what you'll likely find in such a directory:

Federal	**Listed Under**
Social Security Card	Social Security Administration
Veterans' Benefits	Veterans Administration
Section 8	Housing and Urban Development

State	**Listed Under**
Job Openings	Employment Development Department
Apprenticeships	Industrial Relations Department
Worker's Compensation	Industrial Relations Department
Driver's License/I.D. Card	Motor Vehicle Department
Vocational Rehabilitation	Department of Rehabilitation
Paid Training	Workforce Investment Act (formerly JTPA)
Vocational Training	Community College
Post-secondary Education	Community College

County	**Listed Under 'County of'**
Marriage Licenses	County Clerk
Birth/Death Certificates	Health Department
Health Information	Health Department
Alcohol/Drug Abuse	Mental Health Department
Welfare/Medi-Cal	Social Services Department
Child Care Services	Child Care Services Association
Job Openings	Personnel Department
Educational Services	Superintendent of Schools
Vocational Training	Regional Occupational Program

City	**Listed Under 'City of'**
Books, Resource Directory	Library
Community Centers	Parks and Recreation Department
Job Openings	Personnel
Job Openings	Temps, Job Readiness, Day Labor, Ready Labor

Other information found in a telephone book includes:

- emergency phone numbers (fire/ambulance)
- community services
- first aid
- area codes
- time zones
- consumer saving tips
- consumer rights and responsibilities
- yellow pages advertising

Information found in **newspaper** includes:

- help wanted ads (job openings)
- community meetings (Alcoholics Anonymous, etc.)
- telephone hot lines
- church directories
- classified ads

Information found in **community resource directories** include:

- emergency housing
- drug and alcohol abuse centers
- financial assistance
- transportation
- legal assistance
- tax credit programs
- clothing
- food
- WIA (job training)
- counseling (family planning, financial budgeting, marriage and family therapy) medical programs (Medicare, ATP (ability to pay), prepayment plan, dues subsidy plan, and HMO/PPO)
- Workforce Development

U.S. State Abbreviations

The following list of U.S. state and territory (*) abbreviations will be useful when searching the Internet for social services and for referencing addresses throughout this book:

U.S. State/Abbreviations

Alabama - AL
Alaska - AK
American Samoa* - AS
Arizona - AZ
Arkansas - AR
California - CA
Colorado - CO
Connecticut - CT
Delaware - DE
District of Columbia - DC
Federated States of Micronesia* - FM
Florida - FL
Georgia - GA
Guam - GU
Hawaii - HI
Idaho - ID
Illinois - IL
Indiana - IN
Iowa - IA
Kansas - KS
Kentucky - KY
Louisiana - LA
Maine - ME
Marshall Islands* - MH
Maryland - MD
Massachusetts - MA
Michigan - MI
Minnesota - MN
Mississippi - MS
Missouri - MO

U.S. State/Abbreviations

Montana - MT
Nebraska - NE
Nevada - NV
New Hampshire - NH
New Jersey - NJ
New Mexico - NM
New York - NY
North Carolina - NC
North Dakota - ND
Northern Mariana Islands* - MP
Ohio - OH
Oklahoma - OK
Oregon - OR
Palau* - PW
Pennsylvania - PA
Puerto Rico - PR
Rhode Island - RI
South Carolina - SC
South Dakota - SD
Tennessee - TN
Texas - TX
Utah - UT
Vermont - VT
Virgin Islands* - VI
Virginia - VA
Washington - WA
West Virginia - WV
Wisconsin - WI
Wyoming - WY

..

Chapter 2

Support Service Programs

Looking toward the future begins with saying "What is finished is finished. It matters not what happened to me; only what I do with that which happened to me. The next chapter begins with ending the current chapter and beginning anew."

Documentation – Get Copies of Birth and Marriage Certificates

Bureau of Vital Records, State Dept. of Health (Birth/Marriage Certificates):

		Cost
AK	5441 Commercial Blvd, Juneau 99801	$25.00
AL	PO BOX 5625, Birmingham 36103-5625	15.00
AR	4815 W. Markham, Little Rock 72205	12.00
AS	American Samoa Government, Health Info Office, Pago Pago 96799	5.00
AZ	PO Box 3887, Phoenix 85030-3887	varies
CA	PO Box 997410, Sacramento 95899-7410	16.00
CO	4300 Cherry Creek Dr South, HSVRD-VS-A1, Denver 80246-1530	17.75
CT	410 Capitol Ave, Hartford 06134	30.00
CZ	US Dept of State, 1111 19th St NW, Ste 510, Washington DC 20522-1705	30.00
DC	825 North Capitol St NE, Washington 20024 (DC Treasurer)	23.00
DE	417 Federal St, Dover 19901	25.00
FL	PO Box 210, 1217 Pearl St (32202), Jacksonville 32231	19.00
GA	2600 Skyland Dr, NE, Atlanta 30319-3640	25.00
GU	123 Chalan Kareta, Mangilao 96913	5.00
HI	PO Box 3378, Honolulu 96801	10.00
IA	Lucas Office Bldg, 321 East 12th St, Des Moines 50319-0075	15.00
ID	PO Box 83720, Boise 83720-0036	13.00
IL	925 E Ridgely Ave, Springfield 62702	15.00
IN	PO Box 7125, Indianapolis 46206-7125	10.00
KS	Curtis State Office Bldg, 1000 SW Jackson St, Ste 120, Topeka 66612-2221	15.00
KY	275 East Main St 1E-A, Frankfurt 40621	10.00
LA	PO Box 60630, New Orleans 70160	15.50
MA	150 Mt. Vernon St, 1st Fl, Dorchester 02125-3105	28.00
MD	6550 Reistertown Rd, PO Box 68760, Baltimore 21215-0020	12.00
ME	State House Station 11, Augusta 04333-0011	10.00
MI	PO Box 30721, Lansing 48909	26.00
MN	PO Box 64499, St Paul 55164	26.00
MO	930 Wildwood, PO Box 570, Jefferson City 65102-0570	15.00
MS.	PO Box 1700, Jackson 39215-1700	15.00
MT	111 N Sanders, Room 209, Helena 59604	12.00

NC	1903 Mail Service Center, Raleigh 27699-1903	24.00
ND	600 East Blvd Ave, Dept 301, Bismarck 58505-0200	7.00
NE	1033 O St, Ste 130, PO Box 95065, Lincoln 68509-5065	12.00
NH	Archives Bldg, 71 South Fruit St, Concord 03301-2410	15.00
NJ	State Archives, 225 West State St, PO Box 370, Trenton 08625-0370	10.00.
NM	PO Box 26110, Santa Fe 87502	10.00
NV	Capitol Complex, 4150 Technology Way, Ste 104, Carson City 89706	13.00
NY	2nd Floor, 800 North Pearl St, Menands 12204	30.00
NYC	125 Worth St, CN4, Room 133, New York 10013	15.00
OH	246 North High St, 1st Floor, Columbus 43216	21.50
OK	1000 Northeast 10th St, Oklahoma City 73117	15.00
OR	PO Box 14050, Portland 97293-0050	20.00
PA	Birth Unit, 101 South Mercer St, PO Box 1528, New Castle 16103	10.00
PR	PO Box 11854, Fernandez Juncos Station, San Juan 00910	5.00
RI	Room 101, 3 Capitol Hill, Providence 02908-5097	20.00
SC	DHEC, 2600 Bull St., Columbia 29201	12.00
SD	207 East Missouri Ave, Ste 1-A Pierce 57501	15.00
TN	1st Floor, Central Services Blvd, 421 5th Avenue N., Nashville 37243	15.00
TX	PO box 12040, Austin 78711-2040	22.00
UT	288 North 1460 West, PO Box 141012, Salt Lake City 84114-1012	18.00
VA	PO Box 1000, Richmond 23218-1000	12.00
VI	Charles Harwood Memorial Hospital, St. Croix 00820	15.00
VT	PO Box 70, 108 Cherry St, Burlington 05402-0070	10.00
WA	PO Box 47814, Olympia 98504-7814	20.00
WI	1 West Wilson St, PO Box 309, Madison 53701-0309	20.00
WV	Room 165, 350 Capitol St, Charleston 25301-3701	12.00
WY	Hathaway Bldg, Cheyenne 82002	13.00

*U.S. citizens born in a foreign country or high seas, write to:

US Dept of State, 1111 19th St NW, Ste 510, Washington, DC 20522-1705	30.00
*N Mariana Islands: PO Box 500409, Saipan, MP 96950	20.00

Note: Include your name, place of birth – city, county, hospital, if known – date of birth (mo/day/yr), parents' full name, mother's maiden name, purpose of request (lost/destroyed/etc), address (if PO Box, also include physical address), day phone, signature, date of request, and "copy" of I.D. with signature. Make money order or check payable to Vital Records.

Clothing

Excellent resources for inexpensive, quality clothing are American Cancer Society Thrift, Hospice (1-800-646-6460), Salvation Army (www.salvationarmyusa.org), Saint Vincent DePaul (www.svdpusa.org) and other thrift stores. The highest quality items tend to be found at facilities in areas of affluence, places to which affluent people donate.

Domestic Violence

It is a felony for any person to beat, sexually assault, or harm another person, including a spouse. If you are subject of such violence, be sure to contact: National Domestic Violence Hotline at 1-800-799-7233 or (TTY) 1-800-787-3224. www.safenetwork.net. The National Domestic Violence Hotline is 1–800–799–SAFE(7233) or TTY 1–800–787–3224. It's staffed 24 hours a day by trained counselors who can provide assistance and information about shelters, legal advocacy, health care centers and counseling in English and Spanish, and has access to other languages. The Rape, Abuse, and Incest National Network may be contacted at 1-800-656-4673.

Driver's License

Some rules have changed since the 9/11 attacks on the World Trade Center in New York. In some cases driver's license, ID card, and Social Security card can be obtained only after paroling from the institution at which you are incarcerated. Alternatives are being sought. The cost for a driver's license varies by state. To replace a lost or damaged license or to change your name, go to the local motor vehicle department. A regular driver's license is generally issued for a 5-year term. (www.dmv.org)

Financial Aid

- **State-Sponsored-Training and TANF** (Temporary Assistance for Needy Families, a federal assistance program: Replaces AFDC/ADC). State programs provide vocational assessment, employment training and placement. They provide supportive services including work and training related expenses, transportation, and childcare. Aid to Families with Dependent Children provides money for people with children until they are able to support themselves on a rotating on-off basis. Time limits are 18 months for new applicants, 24 months for current applicants. If time limits run out before parent obtains a job, children will continue to receive aid. Examples of support services include domestic violence counseling and transportation assistance, drug/alcohol counseling, and child care services. Recipients of aid are required to pursue a job, or training/education that leads to a job, or to provide volunteer community service, or to provide child care services to other recipients. The Diversion Program eliminates barriers to working (car repairs, work clothes, or tools). Children are required to be immunized and attending school. Drug felons convicted after 1/1/98 and parolees-at-large are not eligible for aid. Welfare fraud results in lifetime denial of aid. Apply at county Department of Social Services. Temporary Assistance for Needy Families (TANF) provides financial aid and services to low-income families with children under the age of 18 who meet the eligibility requirements.

- **General Assistance or General Relief (GA/GR):** This is a county program which helps people with little or no money and those not eligible for other programs. Must be in county and intend to remain there or be unable to travel. Homeless persons should ask eligibility worker about a place to stay. Food and travel vouchers may also be obtained.

- **Social Security (SSI or SSD):** Ex-felons do not automatically qualify; neither number of terms nor addictions are considered. Must be eligible U.S. citizen or non-citizen living in country legally. To get SSI, at least one of the following must apply: 1) age 65 or older; 2) blind; 3) disabled by SSI standards. Note: Doctors chosen by state must confirm disability per strict standards.

Food

- **Brown Bag Program:** For anyone ages 60 or older and low income. Call INFO LINE. Program encourages a small membership fee.

- **Commodity Food/Food Pantries:** Provide free food on an ongoing weekly or monthly basis. The food varies according to government surplus or donations and the frequency it is available varies by county and participating agency. For information call 1-800-273-6222.

- **Congregate Meals:** For anyone ages 60 and over. Spouses of participants can also get meals, no matter what their age. Most sites are located in churches, synagogues, and community centers, but you do not have to be a member.

- **Emergency Food Boxes:** Contain a 3-day supply of food that is generally available the same day it is requested. The amount of food is usually based on the size of the household. Specific requirements such as who is eligible, how often you can obtain, and required documentation vary from county to county. For information, call HELPLINK 1-800-273-6222.

- **Farmer's Market:** Provide fresh products at lower prices directly from farmers and growers.

- **Food Cooperatives:** In the case of SHARE in southern California, you pay $14 or $15 in cash or food stamps and do two hours of community service per month in exchange for a package of food retailing for $30-$40.

- **Food Pantries:** Places that give food to people in need. Operated at churches by volunteers. May require some kind of I.D. and proof that you are low income.

- **Food Stamps:** Food stamps are coupons that can be used to purchase food items. You may be eligible for these even if you work part time or receive unemployment insurance benefits.

- **Gleaners Community Food Bank:** Gleaners gather excess fruit and vegetables following a harvest to feed the hungry.

- **Market Basket:** Provides basket of high quality farm-fresh produce every other week at a cost of $5. Food stamps are accepted.

- **Meals on Wheels:** Meals delivered to those who are homebound. Accept food stamps or small contribution.

- **Parole Food Vouchers:** Based on need, parole officers can give you food vouchers.

- **Project Angel Food:** Delivers free hot meals to homebound people with AIDS.

- **Rescue Mission:** Many communities have Rescue Missions that provide meals in the day and shelter at night. The national directory of local homeless service organizations, listed by state may be search at www.nationalhomeless.org/directories/directory_local.pdf.

- **Summer Food (School) Program:** Children age 18 and under can get free, nutritious meals during the summer or any time when school is out for more than 15 days. Call toll-free 1-800-218-3663.

- **TEFAP Food:** Temporary Emergency Food Assistance Program offers a limited selection of surplus commodities and government-purchased foods to low-income families on a periodic basis (monthly/bimonthly/quarterly) based on your income. Contact Food Bank.

- **WIC:** "Women, Infants, and Children" program provides nutrition counseling, referrals to health care, and food vouchers. Women who breast-feed totally receive an extra set of vouchers. The average value of the vouchers is about $50 per person per month for pregnant women, new mothers, infants, and young children. WIC does not require Social Security numbers or proof of immigration status. Call toll-free 1-888-942-2229.

Housing

1. **Boarding Houses:** Go to the public library or college campus and check the Internet search engine www.google.com or www.infoUSA.com for Boarding Houses for your community. Request a list of boarding houses in the area to which you are relocating and start writing to them.

2. **Churches/Religious Organizations:** Have programs to assist those in need. Inquire with a local church or minister.

3. **County Department of Social Services (DSS):** May have emergency housing. Contact the nearest office and make an appointment.

4. **Delancey Street Foundation:** A residential drug rehabilitation program with an excellent reputation. Delancey Street locations:
   - San Francisco: 600 Embarcadero San Francisco, CA 94107, Tel. 415-512-5104
   - Los Angeles: 400 N. Vermont Ave, Los Angeles, CA 90004, Tel. 323-644-4122
   - New Mexico: P.O. Box 1240, San Juan Pueblo, NM 87566, Tel. 505-852-4291 x304
   - North Carolina: 811 N. Elm St, Greensboro, NC 27401, Tel. 336-379-8477
   - New York: 100 Turk Hill Road, Brewster, New York 10509, Tel. 845-278-6181 x205

5. **Halfway Houses:** Go to the public library or college campus and check the Internet search engine www.google.com or www.infoUSA.com for Halfway Houses or residential drug treatment facilities in your community.

6. **Homeless Shelters:** Go to the public library or college campus and check the Internet search engines, such as www.nationalhomeless.org/directories/directory_advocacy.pdf, www.homelessshelterdirectory.org, www.shelterlistings.org, www.google.com, or www.infoUSA.com, for Homeless Shelters in your community.

7. **HUD:** Department of Housing and Urban Development. Section 8 Rent Subsidies and Public Housing. Most ex-offenders are not categorically banned.

8. **Parole/Probation-Assisted Housing Program:** Many parole/probation offices have contracts with local boarding homes, hotels, or other short-term housing

agencies. Check with your parole agent for information on local nonprofit organizations that also provide food and clothing.

9. **Rental Assistance:** 'Section 8' public housing is aimed at providing housing assistance to low-income people, particularly the working poor. Generally, those on Section 8 pay 30% of their gross income for rent, with the federal government paying the remainder, within predetermined "fair-market" rent levels that change annually. For low-cost rental housing, call the county Housing Authority (HUD) to be put on waiting list for 'Section 8' public housing. Alternative: ask for a 'Section 8 Voucher/Certificate' that will allow you to look for private housing on your own. Housing Authority will pay the difference between cost of rent and what you can afford to pay according to an income sliding scale; the less you make, the less you pay. Salvation Army may assist with payment of deposit or last month's rent, but not of first month's rent; you pay that.

10. **Rescue Missions:** Many communities have Rescue Missions that provide meals in the day and shelter at night. Go to the public library or college campus and check the Internet search engine www.google.com or www.infoUSA.com for Rescue Missions.

11. **Residential Drug Treatment Programs:** Available in most areas. Go to the public library or college campus and check the Internet search engine www.google.com or www.infoUSA.com for Residential Drug Treatment Programs. Also check with your parole or probation agent.

12. **Salvation Army:** Provides residential program for males and emergency housing for women and families. Go to the public library or college campus and check the Internet search engine www.salvationarmyusa.org, www.google.com, or www.infoUSA.com or telephone book for Salvation Army.

13. **Veteran's Administration Housing:** If you are a military veteran, check your eligibility for benefits (training/health care/drug and alcohol treatment/housing/other) with your local veteran's office. Go to the public library or college campus and check the Internet search engine www.va.gov, www.vba.va.gov, www.vba.va.gov/vba/benefits/factsheets, www.google.com, www.infoUSA.com or telephone book for Veteran's Office. NGA.org lists veterans benefits for family support, education, licensing and registration, tax and financial, state employees, and protections, recognitions and employment support. HirePatriots.com connects veterans with opportunities, and opportunities with veterans. The National Veterans Legal Service Program, www.nvlsp.org can assist you in upgrading your military discharge, which may affect your VA Benefits.

14. **YMCA/YWCA:** May provide rooms for single men, for women, or women with children. Check the telephone book for nearest YMCA/YWCA.

Note: Set goals for yourself and develop a workable plan to achieve those goals. If in doubt, ask your parole agent or mentor for programs in your community.

Info-Line (Linea de Informacion)

Info-Line is a telephone information and referral service. You can call 7 days a week, 24 hours per day. Operators are available in many languages. They can help you find a wide variety of resources, including the following:

- Emergency food and shelter
- Legal and financial assistance
- Health services and rehabilitation
- Counseling
- Child care
- Family planning
- Consumer advocacy
- Transportation
- Recreation
- Substance abuse treatment

Hay un servicio de referencias e informacion por telefono llamado "INFO-LINE". Usted puee llamar 7 dias por semana, las 24 horas del dia. Hay operadoras hablan diferentes idiomas. Ellas pueden ayudarle con una gran variedad de recursos comunitarios, incluyendo los siguientes:

- Alimentos y albergue de emergencia
- Asistencia legal y financiera
- Servicios de salud y rehabilitacion
- Consejeria
- Planificacion familiar y cuidado de ninos
- Asesoria para el consumidor
- Transporte
- Recreacion

Call the number listed to reach INFO-LINE if you are in the following areas (Si Ud. Vive en las siguientes areas, llame al numero de informacion): Call 1-800-339-6993. (Si Ud. Vive en una area distinta, llame al 1-800-330-6993.) If you are hearing impaired, call the TDD line at 1-800-660-4026.

(Si esta sordo o parcialmente sordo, llame a la linea TDD al 1-800-660-4026).

They are very busy, but each caller receives good service. Be prepared to wait for the phone to answer; let the phone ring and ring. (Ellos estan muy ocupados, pero se le atendera bien. Debera esperar bastante tiempo para que contesten el telefono; deje que el telefono suene por un largo rato.)

Medical Benefits

1. **Ability-to-Pay (California):** This free or low-cost health plan provides services for low-income people who are not eligible for MediCal or who have medical expenses not fully covered by MediCal, Medicare, and private insurance. ATP charges according to an income sliding scale – the less you make, the less you pay.

2. **Community Clinics:** Available in some counties to serve certain groups of low-income people.

3. **Dues Subsidy Plan:** Certain group health plans (e.g., HMOs like Kaiser North/South) are required to allow a small percentage of low-income families and singles to join at little or no cost.

4. **Healthy Family Program:** For low-income families with children who are uninsured. The program covers doctor visits, hospital care, prescription drugs, emergency care, mental health, immunizations, dental exams and cleaning, and eyeglasses. For information on how to enroll, call 800-747-1222.

5. **HICAP:** Health Insurance Counseling and Advocacy Program. 800-434-0222. HICAP serves current Medicare beneficiaries, persons about to receive Medicare benefits, children or other representatives of Medicare beneficiaries, persons planning for retirement, older persons contemplating the purchase of health insurance, and persons interested in coverage of future health-related costs. HICAP can help you understand your rights as a health care consumer, and Medicare benefits and rights, including how to appeal Medicare claim denials. It can also provide you information on private Medicare supplement health insurance, Health Maintenance Organizations (HMO's), and long-term care insurance.

6. **Lions Club:** Free eyeglasses for children and adults.

7. **Medicaid:** Medicaid is a U.S government sponsored program for low-income individuals and families to pay the cost of health care. For a summary of Medicaid Benefits by state, go online to medicaidbenefits.kff.org/state_main.jsp

8. **Medicare:** The nation's largest health insurance program, which covers nearly 40 million Americans. Medicare is a health insurance program for people age 65 or older, some disabled people under age 65, and people of all ages with End-Stage Renal Disease (permanent kidney failure treated with dialysis or a transplant). (www.medicare.gov)

9. **Miracle Ear Hearing Aid Center:** Free hearing aid for hard-of-hearing children.

10. **Prepayment Plan:** A low-cost, county health care plan. Income, family size, or resources do not have to be proved if you pay the standard fees within 7 days of treatment.

11. **Translators:** As of January 1, 2008 non-public managed care health plans, including most medical, dental, and vision insurance programs, have been required to provide interpreters to communicate orally with subscribers who have difficulty understanding English. Key points:
    - The service is the responsibility of the insurer. Insurers must provide translators regardless of language.
    - Written translation is also required for key languages.
    - To report problems or complaints, call the California Department of Managed Health Care at (888) 466-2219.

12. **Rite-of-Passage: Mankind/Womankind Project:** If you are highly committed to your life and ready to take a hard look at yourself, your deepest fears, your wounds from the past, and the specific ways your life is not working for you, the Mankind Project initiatory work may be for you. This is an invitation to step forward and look in the mirror through group discussions, games, guided visualizations, journaling, and individual process work to discover the meaning of your life. The Mankind Project is an international organization committed to supporting men in their personal development and actively partners with Woman Within, International in offering initiations and trainings for women. For additional information call 1-800-870-4611 or research websites on the Internet.

13. **Social Security Administration (SSA) Benefits:** Some rules have changed since the 9/11 attacks on the World Trade Center in New York. Driver's license, ID card, and social security card can be obtained only after paroling from the institution at which you are incarcerated. Alternatives are being sought. SSA does not issue replacement Social Security number cards to prisoners. You may apply for a replacement card at any Social Security office after your release. Bring two forms of identification (ID). One should be a picture ID such as your CDC card or valid driver's license. If SSA decides it is allowed to issue a replacement card, you will receive a receipt showing your Social Security number. All replacement cards are mailed; they are not issued at local offices. There is no reason to file a claim (application) for SSI payments or Social Security benefits while you are in prison. The law does not permit SSA to pay you while you are in prison. It does not have any way of having a check ready and waiting for you to pick up upon your release. It does not have a "pre-release agreement" with your prison facility. It will not be able to begin processing any SSI claim prior to your prison release date, and it will have to disallow any claim you file before your release. After your release, you may call the toll-free number (1-800-772-1213) to make an appointment to file your claim.

Veterans Benefits Information (www.vba.va.gov)

1. **VA Benefits:** 1-800-827-1000. Education, Home Loan Guaranty, Homeless Veterans' Reintegration Program (HVRP), Disability Compensation, Disability Pension, Dependency Indemnity Compensation, Death Pension, Vocational Rehabilitation and Employment, Civilian Health and Medical Program of the Department of Veterans Affairs (CHAMPVA), Medical Care, Burial, and Life Insurance. Washington D.C. Vet Center Washington D.C. VA Medical Center, 911 Second Street, NE 50 Irving Street, NW, Washington, DC 20002 Washington, DC 20422 (202)543-8821 (202)745-8000. Note: Non-violent ex-felons were recruited for the Armed Forces during several years of the Afghanistan/Iraq War. HVRP: http://www.dol.gov/vets/programs/fact/Homeless_veterans_fs04.htm.

2. **Life Insurance:** 1-800-669-8477.

3. **Education (GI Bill):** 1-888-442-4551.

4. **Health Care Benefits:** 1-877-222-8387.

5. **Income Verification and Means Testing:** 1-800-929-8387.

6. **Mammography Helpline:** 1-888-492-7844.

7. **Gulf War/Agent Orange Helpline:** 1-800-749-8387.

8. **Status of Headstones and Markers:** 1-800-697-6947.

9. **Telecommunications Device for the Deaf (TDD):** 1-800-829-4833.

10. **For health care services,** contact your nearest VA medical facility.

11. **Homeless Veterans Rehabilitation Program (HVRP):** Veterans helping homeless veterans achieve independent living. HVRP offers a clean and sober living

situation, training in skills that help make important lifestyle changes, job assistance, support, and the hope that one can make life work for him or her. HVRP requires a commitment for 4-6 months on a daily basis. Male and female veterans with an honorable or general discharge who are currently without housing or employment. Call 1-800-848-7254 in California, Monday through Friday, 8:00-4:30.

12. **ABS Legal Services LLC:** 1-888-511-9675. ABS legal Services LLC, P. O. Box 3450, Lawrence, Kansas 66046

Chapter 3

Education and Training

THE KEY TO FREEDOM is ongoing education and training, but with that comes responsibilities. Governments provide a great deal of education and training at little or no cost. Grants, scholarships, or loans fund other educational opportunities, especially in the case of private for-profit education and training. Many programs, apprenticeships for example, are learned on the job; you are paid while you learn. While you may believe that education and training are expensive, consider how much the lack of education and training have cost you! And don't forget to calculate the average lifetime earnings of gangbanging and illegal drug sales are – they are than minimum wages when you factor in prison wages.

1. **Adult Education Programs** are free to those seeking a General Educational Development (GED) diploma.

2. **Community Colleges offer** thousands of vocational trades at junior colleges throughout the country. Grants are available to pay the cost (subject to change) per unit tuition, cost of books and tools of vocational training. The maximum Cal Grant A (California only)may be over $8,000; the maximum PELL Grant varies between $400 and over $4,000. Qualification for grants is based on your income for the previous tax year. Those with drug possession/sales may qualify on the basis of having never been convicted for the possession or sale of illegal drugs for an offense that occurred while you were receiving federal student aid (e.g., grants, loans, or work-study). Filling out a FAFSA (www.fafsa.ed.gov) is the first step to applying for thousands of dollars in other financial aid including:

   • State Grant (www.collegescholarships.org/grants/state.htm)

   • Pell Grant

   • Federal Student Education Opportunity Grant (FSEOG)

   • Campus and other aid (check Chapter 13 and 14 for other resources for continuing your education)

3. **Many parole/probation offices** can refer you to Literacy and Vocational Training Programs; inquire about literacy classes that lead to a GED/HS diploma. Many offices can also refer you to vocational training programs in cooperation with county schools and private vendors at a fraction of the typical cost.

4. **Job Corps:** Job Corps is a **free** education and training program that helps young people learn a career, earn a high school diploma or GED, and find and keep a good job. For eligible young people at least 16 years of age that qualify as low income, Job Corps provides the all-around skills needed to succeed in a career and in life. Call (800) 733-JOBS or (800) 733-5627; an operator will provide you

with general information about Job Corps, refer you to the admissions counselor closest to where you live, and mail you an information packet.

5. **Union Apprenticeship Programs:** Apprenticeship training is operated by employers, employer associations, or jointly by management and labor on a voluntary basis. Apprenticeship is structured, comprehensive paid training and related theoretical instruction in occupations that require a wide and diverse range of skills and knowledge, as well as maturity and independence of judgment. It involves planned, day-to-day training on the job and experience under proper supervision, combined with related technical instruction. It may require a high school diploma or GED. Apprenticeship Programs (all counties) are listed below – write to program of your choice or the state office to learn more: State Apprenticeship Office Websites: www.doleta.gov/OA/sainformation.cfm. Some states do not have an apprenticeship website. In those cases, links are provided to the state's Department of Labor website to aid you in contacting the state for more information about apprenticeship programs in that state. Benefits for registered apprentices include: 1) A guaranteed paycheck from day one to increase over time as you learn new skills; 2) Hands-on career training in a wide selection of programs, such as health care, construction, information technology and geospatial careers; 3) Potential to earn college credit, even an associate or bachelor's degree, in many cases paid for by your employer; 4) A successful long-term career with a competitive salary, and little or no educational debt; 5) National industry certification when you graduate that can be taken anywhere in the U.S.; 6) Recognizable partners, such as CVS/pharmacy and UPS, have Registered Apprenticeship programs.

- Air Conditioning/Refrigeration
- Automotive Trades
- Barber
- Boilermaker
- Bricklayers/Caulker/Cleaner/Pointer/Stonemason
- Brick Tender
- Building Inspector
- Butcher/Meat Cutter
- Carpenter/Insulator/Acoustical Installer/Shingler/Scaffold Erector
- Carpet/Linoleum/Soft Tile Installer/Layers
- Cement Mason
- Construction Laborer
- Culinary Worker/Cook
- Drywall/Lather
- Electrician/Inside Wireman/Sound and Communications
- Electrician Construction/Fiber Optics and Television Cable Installer/Voice and Data/Repair Tech
- Elevator Constructor
- Firefighter/Medic/EMT/Paramedic/HazMat/Fire Eqpt/Arson and bomb Investigator/Sprinkler Fitter
- Glazier

- Heat and Frost Insulator/Asbestos Worker
- Heat Ventilation/Air Condition/Insulation
- Ironworker
- Laborers Training and Retraining
- Lineman/Power Lineman
- Machinist (see Auto Trades Machinist)
- Meat Cutter
- Mill and Cabinet Maker
- Millwright
- Operating Engineer/Welder/Diesel Mechanic (Crane-Dredge-Pile Driver-Grader)
- Painter
- Painter, Line
- Patternmaker, Wood (Foundry)
- Pavement Stripper
- Pipe Trades
- Plasterer
- Plumber/Pipe-fitter/Refrigeration Fitter
- Plumber/Steamfitter/Metal Trades Pipe-fitter
- Psychiatric Technician
- Roofer
- Sheet Metal
- Sheet Metal Worker
- State Park Ranger and Lifeguard
- Stationary Engineer/Water Treatment Plant Operator
- Surveyor
- Theatre of Arts
- Tile Layer/Setter
- Tree Trimmer

Entrepreneurial Business Courses – Free Online

The Kutztown University of Pennsylvania Small Business Development Center (SBDC) provides consulting services and educational programs to entrepreneurs looking to start or grow their small business. SBDC consultants may work with entrepreneurs in confidential, one-to-one sessions to help them with a range of business issues including testing a new business proposition, shaping a business plan, investigating funding opportunities, and much more.

SBDC educational programs, in both English and Spanish, serve to inform and assist entrepreneurs with the many decisions a new business owner faces. Program topics range from regulatory compliance issues to marketing tactics and are offered throughout the Kutztown University SBDC service territory with many offerings available online.

A consultant will review your business or proposal, determine a course of action, and identify areas that both of you will be responsible for completing. The consultant will then follow up with an engagement letter detailing your meeting and listing the items both of you will be working on, along with an estimated time frame for completion.

While there is no charge for consulting services, the Kutztown SBDC consulting services differ from consulting firms' services because their clients very actively participate in the work. Generally, the Kutztown SBDC clients use consulting services to guide their process and their thinking; the clients do 80% of the work. The clients rely on the SBDC for guidance, ideas, and feedback from a neutral source as well as for leading edge ideas and resources as they critique their own businesses.

Kutztown University represents one of the largest collections of free, on-demand entrepreneurial resources.

Kutztown University has over 90 online learning programs. It is constantly adding more programs. It represents one of the largest collections of free, on-demand entrepreneurial training resources available in the United States and is part of their "Success Network." It has online learning programs from the SBA, IRS, Small Biz U, Virtual Advisor and custom programs from the Pennsylvania SBDC Network.

The benefits of the online courses to an entrepreneur, small business owner, or start-up business are:

- Learn from the start or brush up on business concepts.
- Courses are available anytime. Watch videos, play, pause, and rewind.
- Current content keeps you updated on business issues.
- Access over 70 business courses, 24/7.
- Become more confident in business environment.
- Increase marketability of your skills and your company.
- Test your knowledge after courses.
- In-depth training on hundreds of today's business issues.

Online courses include: Accounting, Business Operations and Management, Business Planning, Government, Finance, International Business, Legal, Management Development, Marketing, Sales, Small Business, Tax, Starting and Growing a Business.

Read about Kutztown University of Pennsylvania Small Business Development Center (SBDC) at www.kutztownsbdc.org. Contact: Phone (484) 646-4003. Fax (484) 646-4009. Email: SBDC@kutztownsbdc.org

Chapter 4

Employment Supports, Strategies, and Tips

YOU SHOULD BE AWARE of the many programs and services available to help ex-offenders secure employment. Here's what to look for:

- **Bonding:** Federal Fidelity Bonding Program secures the job placement of ex-offenders and other high-risk job applicants. The program functions as a job placement tool by providing employers with a special incentive to hire the hardest-to-place job seekers. http://www.bonds4jobs.com

- **EDD:** Most state Employment Development Department offices have computers with state and nation wide listings. A Job Specialist will assist you. Contact the office regularly and show an interest in working. Note that over two-thirds of all employment is obtained through **friends, relatives, and direct contacts.** Fifteen contacts each day should result in an average of one or more interviews a day. More contacts will result in more interviews. More interviews will result in more job offers. Call your local EDD office or Workforce Investment Board, Private Industry Council, One-Stop or Experience Unlimited (a self-help program for individuals in the professional and technical fields) offices. Check the white pages of the telephone book.

> *Two-thirds of all employment is obtained through friends, relatives, and direct contacts.*

- **Job Corps:** Must be age 16-25 or disabled (no age limit), be legal resident, low income, and have need for education, training, and counseling. To apply, call 1-800-733-5627.

- **One Stop Career Centers:** Offer training referrals, career counseling, job listings, and similar employment-related services. Centers can assist ex-offenders in finding jobs. www.doleta.gov/usworkforce/onestop/onestopmap.cfm. listed by county with address, phone nos., website, and hours.

- **W.I.A./P.I.C./One-Stop Centers:** Provide a one-stop resource for employers and unemployed job seekers, linking them to major employment and on-the-job training programs with wages or classroom training followed by placement in a job as well as other services. Part of wages may be paid by W.I.A. For nearest office, dial 1-800-FOR-A-JOB (1-800-367-2562) and state your Zip Code. Operator will redirect your call.

- **Rehabilitation Department:** Provides services for people with physical, mental, or emotional disabilities who want to become more independent and/or self-supporting. Services include training, job placement, medical treatment, necessary tools, payment for tuition and books, transportation allowances. Many offices have a counselor assigned to help parolees. Follow up with appointments and referrals. Search in white pages of phone book for nearest office.

- **Tax Credit:** Federal Work Opportunity Tax Credit encourages employers to hire ex-offenders by reducing employers' federal income tax liability by as much as $9,000 per qualified new worker. http://www.doleta.gov/business/Incentives/opptax

- A Directory of State WOTC Coordinators can be found at: http://www.doleta.gov/business/incentives/opptax/State_Contacts.cfm
  - **Employers:** Must send certification requests (IRS Form 8850 and ETA Form 9061 or 9062) to their State Workforce Agency (SWA) WOTC Coordinator.
  - **Economic and Community Development Agencies:** Must contact their State WOTC Coordinator to learn how they can help businesses in their area earn Federal income tax savings of up to $9,000 per new hire.
  - **Social Service Delivery and Workforce Development Agencies:** Must contact their State OTC WOTC Coordinator to learn how they can help long-term welfare recipients and 9 other groups of job seekers gain a competitive edge in the job market by qualifying eligible participating employers for this federal tax credit

- **Temps/Day Labor/Job Readiness:** Good resources for temporary jobs that often lead to full-time jobs. Pay is on daily or weekly basis, sometimes accompanied by benefits. Check the business section or yellow pages of phone book. About 40% of temps are eventually hired full-time based on your appearance, dependability, and skills demonstrated. Tandem Employment is an example of a temporary employment agency. It fulfills daily, weekly, monthly, project, seasonal, overtime, and vacation staffing needs. It provides safety equipment, drug and aptitude testing, orientation, uniforms and picture ID. Job classes filled include:
  - **General:** material handlers, loaders and unloaders, and order filers
  - **Construction:** forklift, site prep, job-site cleanup, forms stripping, carpenter's helper, and general labor
  - **Semi-skilled:** machine operators, tradesmen's helpers, shipping and receiving
  - **Factory/Manufacturing:** assembly, quality control, maintenance, inventory, packaging, and machining
  - **Skilled:** drill press, carpenters, and welders
  - **Hospitality:** servers, busing tables, food prep, banquet setup, cleaning, and special event setup)

- **Parole/Probation Departments:** Can link clients to perspective employers and other support services such as financial, shelter, food, clothing, and transportation.

- **Ready4Work Community and Correctional Liaisons:** Must be between 18 and 34 years of age, within 6 months of release from local, state, or federal institutions, or must not have been released longer than 3 months. Must have no record of violent or sexual crimes. Must have clear conduct for one year prior to enrollment in Ready4Work (less for misdemeanants). Must volunteer to participate in the program. Must be willing to arrange payment of applicable fines, restitution, or child support assessments. Must participate in pre- (where applicable) and post-release mentoring. And must be returning or have returned from jail or prison to Los Angeles. Ready4Work prepares returnees to become qualified, skilled workers, and place them in reliable, living-wage jobs.

- **Apprenticeships:** Apprenticeship programs define a formal relationship between an employer and an employee during which the apprentice learns a craft or trade through formalized on-the-job training and related supplemental instruction. Individual programs span a period, of typically 3 to 5 years. Registered apprentices work on the job for 2,000 hours of reasonably continuous employment and attend approximately 144 hours of related and supplemental classroom instruction each year.

- **Operating Engineers Training:** This is a 10-week probationary/orientation training with free room and board and a small weekly stipend. The balance of the apprenticeship training takes place on the job, learning from experienced journeyman operating engineers (6,400 hours), welders or diesel mechanics (8,400 hours).

- **Modoc Railroad Academy:** Railroad training includes intensive program, instructing and educating students in the core fundamentals of railroading. Qualified students receive job placement assistance, including resume preparation, counseling and drug testing to aid in employment. Check online at: www.railroadtraining. com, www.railroaddata.com/rrlinks/Railroad_Training_Programs, and www. modocrailroadacademy.com.

- **Ironworkers:** There's an ongoing need for apprentice ironworkers. Average starting pay is as much as $18/hour plus vacations. Apprenticeship is 4 years. Prerequisites are $285 plus drug test, GED or HS diploma, work boots, helmet, phone, and transportation. Schooling includes 11 Saturdays (7am to 3pm). If you miss one class, it results in termination of apprenticeship. Skills learned are welding, rigging, bolting-up, and structural placement.

- **Teamsters:** The Teamsters hire those with Class-A license. Contact: Program Director in your area or at the national level, www.teamsters.org (202-624-6800). Similar unions: www.tdu.org, www.ibew.org, www.uaw.org, www.afl cio.org.

Top 5 Companies for Minorities

These include McDonald's, Fannie Mae, Denny's, Wal-Mart, and AT&T. Other employers who are known to hire those with felony records include: Swift Transportation (have own training program), Hilton, UPS, Sears, FedEx, Burns Security, Mervyn's, 24-hour

Fitness, 98 Cents Store, Starbuck's, Ace Parking, Red Lion Inn, Marshall's, Goodwill, and Foodlink. Industries include: oil and gas drilling companies, and building and construction trades. About 85 percent of all employers will hire ex-felons. Check with your parole agent or probation officer, if available. He will have _____ a much longer list of employers with whom he works.

Internet Job Search

If you don't have your own computer and Internet connection, you can conduct an Internet job search through an EDD office, a public library, or college campus. It involves searching for federal, state, or local jobs. You can post your resume, explore wages, and locate potential employers, search for schools and colleges, ways to fund your education (PELL), take tests/assessments for apprenticeships or to take traffic school to clear tickets, to search for workforce tools and training. The following are some useful sites:

> *About 85 percent of all employers will hire ex-felons.*

- www.usajobs.opm.gov: USA jobs listings.
- www.usps.com/employment: Posts office job listings.
- www.careeronestop.org: Post resume, explore wages, locate employers, and search for tools.
- www.acinet.org: Employer locator.
- www.Jobstar.org: One of the top-rated job-search websites in Northern California.
- www.Monster.com: Most popular job-search website in America.

Things to Do to Obtain a Job Quickly

1. Ask friends and relatives if there are job openings where they work. These and direct contacts account for 67% of all jobs obtained.

2. Check the 'Help Wanted Ads' in the local newspaper daily and other employment publications.

3. Check the phone book yellow pages and make 15-30 phone contacts each morning. Be prepared to present your name, position desired, years of experience, specific job and transferable skills, and "when may I come in for an interview?"

4. Contact large companies that hire a lot of people and often take applications every day.

5. Contact labor unions and construction site supervisors daily.

6. Contact the County Department of Social Services. You may be eligible for some type of job assistance.

7. Stay in contact with your parole agent. He may have information on employment, on the job training, or other services. Also, you must keep him or her informed of your job status.

8. When applying for employment, have your work history and other information available. Carry your I.D. and Social Security card with you.

9. When interviewing for a job, listen closely and show interest and good manners.

10. Be well groomed when job hunting. Make a good impression. Introduce yourself. State your years of experience using the skills, tools, and equipment in a chosen or related field. Give a statement about specific skills, tools, and equipment. Give a statement about your transferable/universal skills (e.g., problem solving, verbal, etc.). Give a problem-solving statement ("will work overtime, etc."). Give a statement about your self-management skills ("get along with others, etc."). Be ready to give 'proof-by-example' to back up any statement.

11. Do not get discouraged. You only fail when you stop making job contacts. On average, 10-15 contacts generate one interview.

12. It's important to get a job soon. Later, you may decide to pursue a better position that offers better prospects for the future. It's important that you notify your parole agent of any change in your employment status or location within 72 hours; that includes having multiple jobs.

13. Acquire important documents necessary for employment. Most employers require a valid state driver's license or I.D. card. It is important to get one or the other before or immediately after release. Your parole agent may be able to assist you. To get your birth certificate, contact the Vital Statistics Office in the county where you were born. (See page 4-5.) Have it available in case your employer wants a copy.

Job Search Strategies and Tips

Resume

- Effective resumes are clearly worded with specific objective that tells employer exactly what you are looking for.
- Do not mail resumes without a cover letter.
- Most popular resume format that helps mask employment gaps: Functional. Focus on accomplishments and skills. Also good for those changing careers by emphasizing transferable skills.
- Maximum period of time a resume would typically cover: 20 years. Focus on your experiences related to the job you are seeking.
- Recommended number of pages in resume: One and never more than two.

Interviewing

- When to bring up salary in job interview: After you are offered the job.
- When to discuss personal, political or religious matters in job interview: Never.
- Screening techniques you can expect: Testing for drugs or skills.

- When it is acceptable to bad-mouth prior or current employer: Never.
- Key action to take after every job interview: Send a thank-you note.

Job Search

- Length of average job search: 6-12 weeks if not prepared or during a recession.
- Most productive way to find work: Networking through friends, relatives or making direct contact..
- 14 ways to look for work are: direct contacts, family, friends, or professionals (account for over 60% of jobs obtained). Internet, mailing resumes, answering trade journal ads, answering local newspaper ads, private employment agencies, union or other hiring halls, civil service exams, former teachers, Yellow Pages, working with other job seekers, and informational interviews.
- Recommended number of job-search methods you should employ at any one time: 4 and no more than 5.

Social Media and Your Online Behaviour

- Companies have long used criminal background checks, credit reports, and searches on Google and LinkedIn to probe the lives of prospective employees. Now, some companies are requiring job candidates to also pass a social media background check on social media websites – Craigslist; YouTube; Facebook; Twitter; MySpace; Tumblr; Flickr; Picasa; Yfrog; and Photobucket – for online evidence of racist remarks; references to drugs; sexually explicit photos, text messages or videos; flagrant displays of weapons or bombs and clearly identifiable violent activity. Currently, 75% of recruiters are required by their companies to do online research of candidates. And 70% of recruiters in America report that they have rejected candidates because of information online. So, BEWARE of your online presence!

Three Major Employer Expectations

- **Appearance:** Way you look (dress, grooming, and hygiene), behave, write, and speak.
- **Dependability:** Attendance, punctuality, and reliability. Give proof by example of these.
- **Skills:** Transferable or universal, and self-management.

Telephone Goals

- Identify the power person(s) the one who hires and fires.
- Ask for interviews 3 times in response to "Sorry, no openings," such as "I'm very interested in working for your company. When may I call back concerning this position?" "I'm sure my skills will apply to other positions. What positions are available? When may I come in to discuss this with you?" "I understand that there are no openings now, but I would like speak with you about future positions that might open." "Do you know of any companies similar to yours that would be

interested in a person with my skills?"
- Ask for names and referrals.
- Obtain general information about the job and company.
- Check yourself out with the other party: "If you were hiring, would you hire someone with my qualifications?"
- Document results of phone calls.
- Maintain contact with those that appear as good job prospects.

Appropriate Attitudes for Workplace

- Cooperation, maturity, and being open to authority
- Punctuality, enthusiasm, willingness to learn, able to prioritize and achieve goals, able to deal with constructive criticism, and able to organize one's time in most efficient way.

Skills Learned in Crime Applied to Legitimate Pursuits

- **Negatives:** murder, manslaughter, or assault. **Positive Interview Responses:** I have strong confidence level, and am not afraid to speak up or ask questions. I am self motivated, not easily intimidated, not bothered by stress, and can be counted on to get job done.
- **Negatives:** hustling drugs, services, goods or other. **Positive Interview Responses:** I possess good ability to sell, keen marketing sense, and am not easily disappointed. I can talk with people of different ages, backgrounds and educational levels, and know how to close a sale.
- **Negatives:** prostitution and pimping. **Positive Interview Responses:** I work well independently or in a team situation. I follow directions, and am not afraid of hard work. I am creative, have proven sales ability, have an outgoing personality, and am skilled in customer service.
- **Negatives:** fraud and embezzlement. **Positive Interview Responses:** I possess excellent accounting skills, am patient, well organized, and detail-oriented. I have professional demeanor, hands-on computer experience, am a goal-setter, resourceful, and work well with little supervision.

Not Best Qualified? Think Again!

- Research indicates about 65% of the time, the hired employee meets fewer than 50% of the job qualifications. Why? The reason is because job offers are given most frequently to those candidates who, regardless of formal qualifications, sell themselves best, intimidate the least, and listen the most.
- Two-thirds of employers frown on dirty footwear and 60% of employers frown on being late for the interview.

3x5 Job Card

- **Job card,** similar to business card, effectively answers the interviewer's request to "Tell me about you." It appears unique. It quickly hooks the interest of the interviewer. It aids in presenting yourself on the phone or in person. It shows employers that you know what you have to offer. It shows that you are organized and possess important communications skills.

- **Sections of Job Card:**
    - **Name, phone number, target heading:** lets employer know you want a job
    - **Job objective:** this is the job title
    - **Value heading:** alerts employer to your value as a worker
    - **Experience statement:** tells employer what you have to offer
    - **Education statement:** notes how you have prepared for entering the labor market and knowledge to handle the job for which you are applying
    - **Transferable skills:** shows employers that you have more than just a working knowledge of the job
    - **Problem-solving statement:** lets employer know that you are willing to help them solve their problems
    - **Self-management skills:** shows you can get along with co-workers, supervisors, and customers

- **Example of Job (3x5) Card:**

John Doe Home Phone: 313-453-1234   **Message:** 313-782-4321

Position Desired: Carpenter/Cabinet Maker/Laborer/Related

Skill/Experience: Over 5 years of paid/non-paid work and on-the-job training using carpentry skills, tools and equipment. HS/GED graduate with vocational carpentry certificate (1000 hrs. with B average). Can safely operate jointer, planer, assorted hand and power saws, drill presses, lathes, and other tools and equipment. Can design, build, laminate and finish work. Can read blueprints, set trusses and frame. Can meet deadlines, cost out and purchase supplies.

Flexibility: Will work weekends, holidays, overtime, flexible hours, travel up to 50 miles, or relocate.

Personal: I am quality-minded, dependable, career-oriented and organized.

Chapter 5

Anger Transformation

---

*"Resentment is like taking poison and
waiting for the other person to die."*
– Malachy McCourt

ANGER DIRECTLY AFFECTS us all – road rage; domestic violence; habitually angry TV and radio commentators; societies worldwide angry with leaderships; and many modern humans constantly on the verge of mental breakdowns. Anger is a valuable signal and energy source that needs to be channeled and expressed in positive, creative ways. It requires that you distinguish between facts and feelings; facts that are in the eye of the beholder and feelings that results from needs being met or not met. Transformation of your anger can begin with a simple parable: Imagine you are circling a crowded parking lot when, just as you spot a space, another driver races ahead and takes it. Easy to imagine the rage. But now imagine that instead of another driver, a beautiful horse has lumbered into that parking space and settled down. The anger dissolves into bemusement. What really changed? You. In this chapter you will learn about anger myths, the difference between anger management and transformation, the physical harm anger does to your body and that of your children, and how to transform anger creatively, socially, existentially, and spiritually.

Myths of Anger

MYTH 1: Anger is a biochemical-determined event.

REALITY: Stimulation of the brain does not create an aggressive response unless the response was previously learned. A child who is allowed to go to the movies following a tantrum learns to repeat the behavior. A spousal abuser learns to repeat the behavior when he dicerns that abuse works. And children's coping strategies for dealing with stress are acquired through modeling and imitating their parents.

MYTH 2: Anger and aggression are instinctual in man.

REALITY: Except for rare pathologies, the genes do not produce individuals predisposed to violence. Throughout history, status within the group has been achieved by the ability to cooperate. We cry, relax, problem solve, or get angry. We may be predisposed for alcoholism, but this does not guarantee alcoholism, nor provide an excuse to drink. It only provides us information for life management strategies.

MYTH 3: Frustration leads to aggression.

REALITY: Aggression is related to anger arousal plus thought. Frustration only occurs when an expectation, through a memory or wish, is not fulfilled. Men are not angered by mere misfortune but by misfortune perceived as injury. We learn to use anger to express frustration. However, there are many other ways to express frustration – creatively, socially, spiritually, and existentially.

MYTH 4: It's healthy to ventilate.

REALITY: People prone to dump their anger tend to get angrier, not less. Expressing feelings is different from ventilating anger and aggression. Relief from anger can be a learned activity.

Anger Management vs. Transformation

- **Anger management is past-oriented.** It seeks to change the way a person behaves through relaxation, cognitive reframing, humor, talk, redirecting anger, changing the situation, assertiveness training, and problem-solving. Anger management deals with survival and adaptation.

- **Anger transformation is future-oriented.** It seeks to change the way a person thinks within, empowering him to see the world differently, reconfiguring how he relates to the world, as well as how he perceives the world. Anger transformation deals with what makes life meaningful and worthwhile.

Harm Caused to the Body by Anger

- Those who score highest in hostility on a standard personality test are nearly five times as likely to die of heart disease, and four times more likely to die within the next 25 years, as their less hostile peers.

- Anger stimulates the release of adrenaline and cortisol into the bloodstream. Adrenaline mobilizes the body over the short term for flight or fight, but can be destructive if anger is chronic, often leading to heart disease, according to research. Adrenaline causes the heart rate and blood pressure to rise. Increased cortisol depresses the immune system, making us more susceptible to illness and slow to recover.

- Anger causes increased testosterone and cortisol that can damage the delicate inner lining of the arteries and accelerate the development of arteriosclerosis, which increases coronary artery disease, and may lead to a heart attack.

- Increased epinephrine and norepinephrine shunt blood from skin, liver, and digestive tract and to heart, lungs, and skeletal muscles. When the liver is less effective, it does not clear cholesterol from the body as well. Fatty deposits are left in the arteries.

- Anger causes platelets circulating in the blood to become sticky, cling to damaged areas on the artery lining, where they clump and release chemicals thought to further stimulate the growth of arteriosclerotic plaque.

- Anger stimulates fat cells to empty into the bloodstream to provide a quick energy source. When that fat is not burned, it is converted into cholesterol that may be incorporated into plaque.

- Anger causes the heart muscle to become larger and less efficient.

- Anger increases secretions of hydrochloric acid, leading to increased gastritis, ulcers, and ulcerative colitis.

Harm Caused to Children by Anger

- Anger is particularly destructive around children. Putdowns affect children's self-esteem and effectively lower their IQ by as much as 25 points.

- Anger adversely affects children's problem-solving ability by as much as 30 points. Imagine an explosive session of anger during breakfast followed by parents sending their children off to school and expecting them to do well.

- An anger-oriented environment often leads to a harmful imbalance of cortisol in a child's brain, resulting in cognitive and developmental delays, memory lapses, anxiety, and an inability to control emotional outbursts.

- Children may also experience chronic elevated resting heart rates, body temperature, and blood pressure that simply do not come down.

- In the case of neglected children, research shows an average of 20 percent smaller cortexes in the brain, or the thinking part of the brain. Abused and neglected children also run a high risk of developing mental illnesses, attention deficit hyperactivity disorder (ADHD), and a decline in their IQ over time.

What is Rational Emotive (Cognitive) Behavior Therapy (REBT)?

REBT is an effective, short-term and low-cost program. It works best for individuals desiring a scientific, present-focused, and active treatment for coping with life's difficulties. It is based on a few simple principles having profound implications (www. threeminutetherapy.com/rebt.html):

- **You are responsible for your own emotions and actions.** Only you can upset yourself about events; the events themselves, no matter how undesirable, can never upset you. Neither another person nor adverse circumstances can ever disturb you; only you can. No one else can get into your gut and churn it up. Others can cause you physical pain or block your goals. But you create your own emotional suffering, or self-defeating behavioral patterns, about what others do or say.

- **Your harmful emotions and dysfunctional behaviors are the product of your irrational thinking.** Over 87 percent of all self-talk is negative; and over 87 percent of all illnesses appear to be psychosomatic, that is, self-induced through negative self-talk.

- **You can learn more realistic views and, with practice, make them a part of**

you. Anger is an addictive habit, most often learned in early childhood from our caregivers. Negative habits can be replaced by positive habits through long-term practice, and practice makes for improvement, not perfection.

- **You'll experience a deeper acceptance of yourself and greater satisfactions in life by** developing a reality-based perspective. This begins with identifying your "musts." Once you admit that you distort your own emotions and actions, then determine precisely how. The culprit usually lies in one of the three core "musts."

    1. **Demand on self:** "I *must* do well and get approval, or else I'm worthless." This demand causes anxiety, depression, and lack of assertiveness.

    2. **Demand on others:** "You *must* treat me reasonably, considerately, and lovingly, or else you're no good."

    3. **Demand on situations:** "Life *must* be fair, easy, and hassle-free, or else it's awful." This thinking is associated with hopelessness, procrastination, and addictions.

Inward Anger vs. Outward Anger

- **When anger is turned inward,** it will be disguised as self-loathing, passive aggression, sarcasm, and, rarely, suicide. Held in, it is susceptible to depression and explosive outbursts.

- **When anger is turned outward** and directed toward others, it may result in being fired, divorce, road rage, vandalism, and random violence that may lead to traumatized family members, jail, or prison.

Anger Transformed Creatively

Anger may be transformed creatively through artistic works, scientific inventions, new products, poems, short stories or novels written, or musical scores played. When imagination is fueled and powered by anger, anything is possible. The creative process and the embracing of creative values can be constructive rather than destructive. Some of the most creative and beneficial endeavors have come out of the depth of pain, suffering, and anger. List five ways that you can commit to creatively transform your anger:

1. _____
2. _____
3. _____
4. _____
5. _____

Practice makes for improvement, so consciously practice transforming your anger creatively until it becomes a habit.

Anger Transformed Socially

Anger may be transformed socially through community activism and political struggle. Social interest and acts of altruism can indirectly reduce one's angry feelings. Social transformation can be an individual or group effort, galvanized and organized to overturn an injustice or to fight for freedom rather than continue to be a "model" citizen whose rights have been abused or removed. List five ways that you can commit to socially transform your anger:

1. _____
2. _____
3. _____
4. _____
5. _____

Practice makes for improvement, so consciously practice transforming your anger socially until it becomes a habit. Resignation, cynicism, and bitterness can fester and destroy a person. But smothering anger can also spark the spirit of reformation to fight against injustice, oppression, and abuse.

Anger Transformed Spiritually

Anger may be transformed spiritually through transcendental experiences such as prayer, meditation, forgiveness, and reconciliation. We perceive that we are no longer alone in our efforts to control anger, because we can solicit divine help according to our unique beliefs and faith traditions. Anger is transcended and gives way to praise when spirituality is an important part of our lives. But spiritual transformation, as well as attitudinal values, must be embraced by the person first before it can be practiced effectively. So, begin by listing five ways that you can commit to spiritually transform your anger:

1. _____
2. _____
3. _____
4. _____
5. _____

Practice makes for improvement, so consciously practice transforming your anger spiritually until it becomes a habit.

Anger Transformed Existentially

Anger may be transformed existentially with wisdom, serenity, and a higher purpose through enlightened acceptance, detachment, and self-transcendence. Anger can awaken the defiant human spirit and propel one to heroic efforts in serving a cause greater than oneself. Embracing attitudinal values enable a person to discover meaning and set one free from self-pity and self-destruction perpetuated by anger, aggression, addiction, and depression. List five ways that you can commit to existentially transform your anger:

1. _____

2. _____

3. _____

4. _____

5. _____

Practice makes for improvement, so consciously practice transforming your anger existentially until it becomes a habit.

Chapter 6

Health Through Meaning:
The Power of Logotherapy

*"Ultimately, man should not ask what the meaning of his life is,
but rather must recognize that it is he who is asked.
In a word, each man is questioned by life; and he can
only answer to life by answering for his own life;
to life he can only respond by being responsible."*
– Viktor Frankl, *Man's Search for Meaning*

LOGOTHERAPY, OR HEALTH through meaning, has been used successfully in dentistry, with doctors and nurses, in religious counseling, groups, and marriage counseling, with the young, old, and those with various addictions, with criminal offenders, on the job, and in a variety of community arenas. It focuses on the most powerful motivating and driving force in humans: the pursuit of meaning in one's life. It is a life philosophy as well as a therapeutic healing approach, with emphasis on the **reality of the spiritual**. The spiritual dimension is the medicine chest that maintains health and helps restore health.

When we lack meaning in our life, we feel a void and frustration. We occasionally hurry to fill that void. We achieve an adrenaline rush and temporary relief. With no apparent alternative, we repeat what appears to work, leading to addictions, underemployment and bankruptcy, divorce, and depression.

Viktor Frankl emphasized that **life has meaning under all circumstances** – yes, even incarceration. He should know. Frankl described in his book, *Man's Search for Meaning,* of having been thrown into prison, stripped of his clothes, all worldly possessions, and shaven. Others had their gold and silver implants removed from their teeth. Frankl's pregnant wife was forced to have an abortion. His mother, father and brother were also thrown in prison. Later, all of his family members, except for a sister who was able to escape, died by starvation or poisonous gas. Despite the horrors and hardships he experienced, Frankl continued to embrace the belief that his life still held meaning. As I noted in the Introduction, the belief in experiential values holds that **all experiences, encounters, and loves benefit us in some way**, especially those that may be traumatic and unavoidable. Creative values require that we pursue that which gives meaning to our life; if I am a writer, I must write; if I am a musician, I must produce music. Having certain skills and being able to put them into practice makes our life meaningful. Frankl was able to forgive those who robbed him of his family, noting that life still had meaning for him He believed each of us is responsible for "what we do, whom we love, and how we suffer." He felt that people find meaning through action, love, and suffering. People need tasks to keep life worth living. He considered love "the ultimate and highest goal to which one can aspire," and says, "The salvation of man is through love and in love."

In his book, *The Pursuit of Meaning*, Frankl says that suffering can lead to growth. He does not encourage pain and suffering, noting that needless suffering is merely masochistic. Instead, he suggests finding meaning in unavoidable suffering. Frankl emphasizes that our attitude always remains under our control, even when our life circumstances are not. Suffering has meaning, in Frankl's view, if it "changes the sufferer for the better."

Frankl sees life's purpose as **self-transcendence** (becoming more) rather than self-actualization (which he sees as allowing what one is). "…Happiness, contentment, peace of mind and self-actualization are mere side products in the search for meaning." Frankl envisions health not as a tensionless equilibrium, but a striving and searching. In this process, we may confront conflicts between values.

> *People find meaning through action, love, and suffering. They need tasks to keep life worth living.*

You are not your mistakes. You are a survivor, not a helpless victim. **You always have choices**, even if only choices of attitude. During the transition from incarceration to parole or freedom without parole, **begin to make responsible and meaningful choices**. Take steps, no matter how small. Also, accept societal responsibilities and commitments, and begin to make changes.

Once you have gained some distance from addiction, aggression, and depression, it becomes easier. The transition from incarceration to parole is the time to discover your meaning potential – your life purpose. **Strive to discover that which gives meaning to your life**. It can simply be labor, or mechanical work, music, or writing, speaking, or creating.

As you gain increasing distance between what was and what can be, you become increasingly empowered with **new attitudes**. What may have appeared unbearable now seems manageable **without** self-medicating. This is also a time to obtain feedback from others about your attitude shift that helps solidify the changes that you have made.

This is also a time to enhance your future health. Write or discuss potential meanings in your life that you have newly discovered. Learn to accept and work through value conflicts and frustrations. Learn to accept responsibility. Look for meanings in your world that previously went unnoticed and circumstances in order to cope more effectively with the world.

This is also a time to begin listing your short-, medium-, and long-range life goals, aims, and ambitions. Devote a few minutes each morning and night **visualizing these**

goals, what they would look like once accomplished. Visualizing is a process of moving toward and becoming your dreams and goals. Remember, obstacles are only little monsters one sees when one takes his eyes off his goals. You do not need to barrel your way through obstacles; there are alternatives.

The Initial Transition

Everybody has strong points of personality, good luck, and successes in life. Individuals also have weak points of personality and circumstances, bad luck, and failures in life.

This is a time to recognize specific life problems that have caused you trouble or internal conflict. They may have been the result of something you did, something someone else did, or due to some sort of fate or destiny. You may have had a life-long dream of what you really wanted to become in life. Make a list of how you expect to work on fulfilling your hopes, on becoming what you want to be in life. Along the path, summarize your progress and give thanks in all things, regardless of whether it was positive or negative. Develop a habit of thinking positively by imaging, then acting positively as if you were the successful, self-confident, capable person you would like to become by doing, not just trying, at least one thing such a person would do.

> *A group of men incarcerated at San Quentin Prison formed a logotherapy support group – a logo-group. The rate of recidivism: 5 percent!*

Find your purpose in life through volunteer work, educational classes, aptitude and interest tests, encounter groups, meditation or spiritual encounters, and physical exercises. Volunteer to be a mentor of at-risk youths. Volunteer in a project for the homeless. Find your purpose in life through exploring human values for personal meaning, and special activities in the search for creative values. Form a "logo-group" based on the principles of logotherapy. Observe how others have found a purpose in life. Find a meaningful cause for which to work.

Describe something to do, someone to love, and something to hope for. List meaningful experiences you gained from the world of events. Describe the spiritual significance of your own life. Think back over your own life to some inescapable circumstance you had to face and write how it has become a gift. Describe an achievement that others held little hope of you achieving – for example, achieving an educational goal, or opening a successful business. Describe your three most important goals in order of importance:

1. _____

2. _____

3. _____

Meaning-Support Groups

Viktor Frankl often corresponded and spoke with men incarcerated at San Quentin Prison. His close friend and fellow Holocaust survivor, Joseph Fabry, conducted two round-table discussions on logotherapy at Folsom State Prison. Frankl noted that a group of men incarcerated at San Quentin Prison formed a logotherapy support group prior to their release – a logo-group. Following their release, they continued the support group, meeting once a week or month. All but one of the men in the original Logo-Group remained free. The rate of recidivism: 5 percent! Consider the fact that the odds of a child ending up in the judicial system, if he is a child of a recidivist parent, are about 92 to one when compared to children whose parent(s) has never been in prison. Those are gambling odds you never want to validate!

But Life is Unfair

Imagine losing a one-year-old child. Imagine losing a spouse after six months of marriage. You would perhaps feel depressed and view your life as not having any meaning. However, consider that fact that those 12 months of watching your baby grow, her first smile, words, rolling over and crawling, and first steps toward you, or those six months of marital bliss can never be taken from you. Nothing and nobody can ever remove those treasures, those meaningful gifts. Even if you should remain single, your life can never become meaningless once your peak experiences of love have been stored in the storehouse of the past, a novel of a life greater than any that has ever been written! "The most pathetic person in the world," notes blind and deaf Helen Keller "is someone who has sight but has no vision." She emphasizes that "although the world is full of suffering, it is also full of overcoming of it."

> *"The most pathetic person in the world is someone who has sight but has no vision."*
> *– Helen Keller*

Logotherapeutic Aphorisms

- The rules of life do not demand that you win at any price, but that you not give up the fight.
- You cannot influence fate, but you can master it through the attitude you adopt.
- When you panic seeing old doors being shut, realize that there are new ones opening.
- The tension between what you are and what you ought to be makes for mental health.
- The "novel" a person has lived is an incomparably greater creative accomplishment than any written one.
- It does not matter what you expect of life; what counts is what life expects of you.

"A man who becomes conscious of the responsibility he bears toward a human being who affectionately waits for him, or to an unfinished work, will never be able to throw away his life. He knows the 'why' for his existence, and will be able to bear almost any 'how'." *– Viktor Frankl*

The Intensive Journal® – A Tool for Discovering Meaning

A Simple System

The following is a brief description of the *Intensive Journal®*. It in no way is a substitute for participating in workshops provided by a facilitator through the Dialogue House who enable you to use the very empowering tool. In a study of over 50 men who participated in at least one workshop, not one returned to prison over a 10-year period. Putting your day-to-day thoughts in writing automatically forces you to become more introspective. This helps you identify patterns in conscious and unconscious thinking. As you work in your journal, the experiences of your life – times of exaltation and despair, moments of hope and anger, crises and crossroads, failures and successes – will gradually fit into place. You will discover that your life has been moving **forward** to destinations you may have been unaware of. You need not believe that you must write something in each section of your journal each day. You will want to write in some sections quite frequently; others may be saved for special occasions. Although you should write in your journal as often as possible, writing should never be a chore. Once you have established a dialogue with your journal, your inner self will tell you when there are things to be written, and you will naturally turn to your journal as a means of self-expression and self-discovery.

Period Log

This is where you will make your first entry each time you write. Write about things that are going on in your life **now.** Now can be a short or a long period of time. It may, for example, reach back three years since you were involved in an automobile accident and were hospitalized. It may be merely a few weeks since you were informed of divorce proceedings, or of the sudden death of a loved one or close friend. Ask yourself: "Where am I now in my life?" Write in a non-judgmental way.

Twilight Imagery Log

After you complete your basic entry in the period log, try to duplicate the twilight state between sleeping and waking. Sit quietly in a comfortable position with no outside sensory disturbances. Relax with eyes closed; follow your breathing until you feel a great calm. On your mental screen, picture a deep cavern. Enter the cavern and go deeper and deeper. At the bottom of the cavern is a river. The waters are muddy but they begin to clear. Examine the images that appear. Then allow yourself to become a bit more alert and jot those sensory images down, be they visual, auditory, tactile, or other sensory images. Then return to the **Twilight State**; keep moving back and forth jotting down the sensory images. Ask yourself if the symbolic images suggest anything. No matter how strange or silly, make a note or picture of it.

Daily Log

These entries should focus on the emotions you experienced during the day. Include only a minimum of descriptive material. The primary purpose of the daily log is to provide ideas for other sections of the journal. Example: If you mention your addiction in the daily log, you might want to talk with it in the upcoming **Dialogue** section.

Steppingstones

Draw a map of your life, an autobiographical sketch that only includes short 'chapter headings' from the beginning to the present that includes eight to 12 significant emotional events – ups and downs and main events – that have shaped your life. Include important times in your life from childhood onward, such as significant school events, your first love, a marriage, divorce, parenthood, friendship(s), and relocation(s). Explore the periods when possibilities were opening for you, when you had alternatives, when critical decisions were made or unmade. Extend your map into the future. No drawing skills are required or expected. Don't pay attention to how well you draw, but let forms, shapes, symbols, and colors flow from your unconscious. Don't plan ahead. Let things happen. Use a sheet of paper and colored pens or crayons, if available. Don't judge yourself. Draw neutral observations about your life. The purpose is to recreate in the present the exact feelings you had when you were going through a momentous time. Steppingstones made us who we are today. Begin by listing the key events. When you have completed the list, go back over the list and number them sequentially as to when they took place. Finally, if you are able to, state the gifts of these events, that is, how each may have benefited you. (Note: You may not have yet realized how you were benefited and that is okay. Simply state: "This has benefited me by _____." Fill in the blank when it appears to you.)

Life History Log

When you do not want to be sidetracked form the section you are working in, but want to retain a memory that has arisen, or a dream that is remembered, record the thought briefly in this section. This will become a grab bag of memories that do not fit anywhere else.

Intersections: Roads Taken and Roads Not Taken

Record here those experiences that marked an intersection in your life, where some kind of change became inevitable. The choices you made at those intersections left many potential paths untouched and unexplored. Although those unlived possibilities have never been given their chance, you may still be waiting for an opportunity to do so. Example: You got married instead of pursuing an career in heating and air conditioning, or you took a corporate job instead of starting your own business, or you sold illegal drugs instead of beef jerky as a telemarketer. Ask yourself: Can any of these roads still be traveled? How do you feel about doing it now?

Dialogues With...

Having begun by recording and exploring much of your life history, it is time to deepen your relationship with the important aspects of your life – persons, works, finances, body, and dreams – and let them speak to you. Write down what is or was positive or negative about your relationship with that aspect of your life, how it got to where it is and what your hopes are for it. Next, as best you can, list eight to 12 **steppingstones** for that person or part of your life. Do the twilight imagery meditation. Then write a dialogue where you express what you really mean to each other. Listen carefully to what the other part – living or dead, animate or inanimate, spiritual or material – has to say to you.

You may "dialogue with a person" who may be living or dead, with whom you had an important relationship. Example: In a dialogue with your deceased father you may ask, "Why did you beat me so much? Didn't you ever really love me?" He may respond, "I did. I was just too messed up and too busy to express my love for you..."

You may "dialogue with work," listing the kinds of work you have done in your life. State the situation you find yourself in regarding that kind of work, and listen to what the work has to say. Example: You may talk to the bills you've been avoiding. The bills may respond, "You do not want to pay us because you want to be a kid, irresponsible and have somebody else pay."

You may "dialogue with body," listing two or three important physical events for each decade of your life; then, relaxing and writing a conversation with that part of your body. Example: "When I was young, I could drink as much alcohol as I wanted and bounce back quickly. Now I can't seem to hold down a job or retain a relationship."

NOW: The Open Moment

This section is about your future. First, sum up your experiences writing in this journal. Then, focus on your future in the context of your life history. Write whatever comes to you. It may be a prayer, a poem, a brief focusing phrase, or a picture that gives you a reminder about the continuity of your life.

Again, although journaling is important, do not feel that you have to write each and every day. What is important is that you are writing...and, in doing so, learning more and more about the direction your life is taking, about you, and the "meaning of the moment."

To learn where Intensive Journal workshops are being held, contact Jon Progoff at Dialogue House, 2155 Ocean Avenue, Suite C, Ronkonkoma, NY 11779; 631-471-0542; or www.IntensiveJournal.com.

Chapter 7

Positive Parenting Principles

Old Woman in a Shoe

"There was an old woman who lived in a shoe.
She was a kindhearted mom who knew exactly what to do.
She raised all her children with patience and love.
Never once did she give them a spank, shake or shove.
Her children all learned to be gentle toward others.
And good parents too when they became fathers and mothers.
From their days in the shoe they learned this about living:
Kindness, not force, is the gift that keeps giving."
– Jordon Riak

YOU CAN LEARN a lot about yourself and your own parenting skills from the Old Lady in the Shoe! While parenting is by no means easy, it's especially difficult for those who lack a sense of personal responsibility, possess little knowledge about the basics of effective parenting, and are often absent fathers or mothers.

Many ex-offenders need to strengthen their **parenting skills**. In fact, parenting is often a life-transforming experience where personal responsibility takes center stage. Interesting things happen when they become parents. Attitudes and outlook on life change as you learn about the challenges of parenthood. Fatherhood and motherhood require taking responsibility for loved ones and helping them shape an exciting and meaningful future. Accordingly, many ex-offenders acquire greater meaning in their lives as well as become more responsible people when they become parents. Here are some inside tips on how to become a more effective and responsible parent.

Tips to Decrease Parent/Child Power Struggles

1. Use routine, not your mouth: Set up a clear, daily structure beforehand. Cut down on verbal commands. If words are necessary, choose them wisely and sparingly.

2. When you can't change the child, change the environment: Make concrete changes in the physical setup of the household so that it dictates the rules, while your child enjoys some independence.

3. **Follow up with follow-through:** Carefully choose routine and rules that rely on your follow-through, not your child's. Let the consequences be your child's reminder and your salvation.

4. **Stay grounded with ground rules:** Stick with non-negotiable rules to retain your credibility and to keep your children from breaking you down with their use of logic and reason.

5. **Negotiation creates cooperation:** When you create rules with your children they are more likely to view them as positive tools for order and to cooperate.

6. **Reduce children's tasks to manageable size:** Build your children's self-esteem by providing them with tasks that are age-appropriate. Focus on seemingly insignificant activities that fill every child's play.

7. **Emphasize your children's responsibilities:** Balance your decision to hand responsibility back to your children, but with a supportive caring attitude.

8. **Treat your children as a part of the family team:** Sibling relationships are a great place to teach your children to be cooperative team players. During sibling rivalry and fights, do not show favoritism by taking sides. Instead, encourage them to problem solve and learn important relationship skills.

9. **Teach your children how to resolve conflict:** Conflict is a part of almost every child's play, a part of learning and development. Use distraction by introducing a craft activity such as repairing broken toys to give to needy children. Engage them in talk about compromise and sharing. Initiate a time-out while they come up with solutions to get along better. Help them to understand the feelings of others by letting each child air his grievances without being interrupted. Then, let the other children paraphrase what they heard. Give your children the tools to understand the problem and to compromise. Help them to calm themselves with calming techniques such as deep breathing, or humor. Sidestep unnecessary struggles in a way that won't put your children on the defensive. When you avoid your own defensive maneuvers, your children will have no need for theirs.

10. **Make points with action, not emotion:** Emphasize your point with action. You can walk, point, or even use pantomime without hurtful or angry words as you move away from the power struggle.

11. **Correct behavior with a connection:** Make a connection between the child's misbehavior and the resulting discipline. Whenever possible, let your children experience the results of his/her behavior.

12. **Stick with consequences:** Be consistent and teach with consequences even when it seems easier and quicker to not follow through.

13. **Make the most of inconsequential positive moments:** The key to being encouraging even in the hardest of times is to realize the importance of the simple, everyday happenings that are all too often ignored. So, open your eyes and ears, and celebrate those positive moments of your children sharing, encouraging one another, and being loving.

14. **Tune in to your children's need for attention:** Instead of always working so hard at making your children understand what you say, work hard at understanding and acknowledging what they say and do.

15. **Make your children aware of their accomplishments:** Rather than focus on your child's potential to boost his/her morale, bring to light their valuable, irrefutable accomplishments by describing what they see and remembering past, mastered accomplishments, no matter how small.

16. **Emphasize learning experiences of failures that accompany small successes:** While it is okay to praise performance, you can multiply your self-esteem builders by highlighting the many small successes that occur as your child tackles each task. Point out the positive learning experiences of failures.

17. **Be present for your child.** Ultimately, to discipline a child is to make him/her your disciple, a responsibility that requires you to be present for your child's needs 24/7 physically and emotionally.

18. **Be your child's first and most powerful teacher.** Family relationships, practices and patterns of life are a more powerful predictor of academic learning than a family's economic status. www.leapfrog.com provides endless ways to play with your children as they discover something new every day. www.khanacademy.org provides video-taped presentations of virtually every school subject from elementary school to college level in a stimulating, language-rich, supportive environment

Alternatives to Shaking, Hitting, Spanking, Yelling, Threatening, and Putting Down

Face it: adults do not possess an instinct for parenting. Even parenting classes do not agree with one another. Consequently, children are often the unfortunate recipients of momentary parental anger, frustration, and an overall temporary sense of incompetence as parents. This feeling is magnified when parents follow the old, standby rule "spare the rod, spoil the child" and discover to their frustration that, in general, psychological research proves it does not work. Proof that it does not work is the fact that it must be repeated and, sadly, increased in severity.

What we do know from research is that continued violence toward children has **no** long-term positive or beneficial influence on them. On the contrary, yelling, threatening, and putting down children negatively affects their self-esteem and effectively lowers their IQ by as much as 25 points. It also adversely affects their problem-solving ability by as much as 30 points. When a child grows up in an anger-oriented environment, the adrenaline rush is constant. This often leads to a harmful imbalance of cortisol in the brain, resulting in cognitive and developmental delays, memory lapses, anxiety, and an inability to control emotional outbursts. Research also observes that neglected children have an average of 20 percent smaller cortexes in the brain, or the thinking part of the brain. All these factors taken together, children are sent off to school and expected to succeed!

Children, when given a choice between positive and negative attention, will generally choose the positive attention of being treated as a human being of worth, love, and kindness. On the other hand, when given a choice between negative and no attention (neglect) they will generally choose the negative attention. Negative attention is better than no attention! In fact, children who are victims of repeated corporal punishment often have lower self-esteem and self-concept, are less secure, less happy, and feel less positive about others and the world in general. In the absence of positive attention, negative behaviors continue to increase in frequency in order to garner the negative attention.

> *Yelling, threatening, and putting down children negatively affect their self-esteem and effectively lower their IQ by as much as 25 points.*

Children who are reared by supportive, accepting parents with whom they can identify tend to develop into self-aware adults capable of formulating long-term goals. They often engage in constructive self-criticism and cherish their relationships with others. In contrast, children whose parents are overly critical, harsh, or authoritarian often turn into self-absorbed and impulsive adults whose impulsiveness can lead them to violence and substance abuse (*Child Development*, Vol. 58: 859-869.1987).

"The recidivist male delinquent who has never been exposed to a belt, board, extension cord or fist at some time in his life is virtually nonexistent. As the severity of corporal punishment in the delinquent's developmental history increases so does the probability that he will engage in a violent act." (Ralph Welsh, Ph.D. Psychologist)

With lasting memories and feelings, the perpetuation of corporal punishment is passed from one generation to the next. For the most part, we are a product of the way we are treated by the significant others in our world. When grown-ups who were spanked spank their own children, they are activating their unconscious need to pass the humiliation on. "What was good enough for me is good enough for my child." There is nothing loving about the act of hitting someone who is five times smaller than you are, even if you do it with the best of intentions. (www.nospank.net)

Our parents and grandparents were not bad for spanking us. They were uninformed. They drove Model T's. We don't do that any more. They grew up in homes painted with lead-based paint. We no longer do that. They jumped off high rock cliffs into dangerous rivers. Well, we continue to do that! Those who quote the Bible to justify their honest beliefs forget that the Bible makes its harshest judgment on those who hurt little children." (John Bradshaw on spanking, from "The Bradshaw Connection," broadcast on November 22, 1996, WOR-TV)

Somehow or some way, sooner or later, the developing low self-esteem and low self-concept, as well as inward feelings of anger, insecurity, and distrust, will be (fear) directed outward toward society. An old African proverb says, "If you do not (positively) initiate the youth, they will burn down the village." Personal violence will not be denied until we sincerely believe and want to work toward eliminating violence toward children and one another.

Positive Attention and Discipline Help Children to

1. Think
2. Learn so that their present behavior is changed
3. Grow intellectually and morally, enhancing their self-confidence and self-image
4. Learn a lesson that will carry over and positively affect future behavior
5. Fit into the family and society in a comfortable way that leads them to conclude that they are basically good, strong, and effective persons
6. Control and change their behavior, thereby guiding them into adulthood

Negative Attention and Discipline Diverts Children

1. Toward negative behavior, such as rebelliousness, aggressiveness, and destructiveness
2. Toward using drugs and alcohol to replace other pleasures of life
3. Toward stealing to replace work in obtaining his or her 'wants'
4. Away from ability to deal with or to express feelings
5. Toward increasingly displaying negative behaviors in order to be the center of attention

Responding to a Crying Baby

When you are tired and your baby's crying, the most important thing is to keep a positive attitude. When babies cry, they're communicating. The cry is a universal language telling you they need something. Make up your mind that you're there to help your baby, not necessarily to stop her from crying. Once you've got the right attitude, it's easier to stop yourself from hurting your baby in frustration of not knowing the language. Pediatric researchers have discovered that babies around the world "speak" the same universal language, communicated through the unique sounds of their "crying." The following are five of the basic sounds and their meaning, made by a newborn up to about six months when crying:

Sound	Meaning
Neh	"I'm hungry." This sound is based on the strong sucking reflex of a newborn combined with a cry. When this sound is heard, it's time to nurse or to give your newborn a bottle.
Owh	"I'm sleepy." This sound is based on the yawning reflex. The first "owh" sound can be long and pronounced. When this sound is heard, help your baby go to sleep. The more tired babies become, the harder it is for them to go to sleep. Look for other clues such as rubbing of eyes and yawning.

Heh	"I'm feeling discomfort." This sound is different than the "I'm hungry" cry; there is a strong "h" sound at the beginning. If you hear this cry in your newborn, s/he may need her/his diaper changed or be put in a new position.
Eair	"I have lower gas." When babies have lower gas pain, they often pull their legs towards their chest and make this sound. When newborns have gas, they like a bit of pressure on their tummies, massaging with slow circular motions. Lay them on your legs perpendicularly and rub their backs or hold them in the elbow of your arm with your elbow supporting their head and their legs straddling your arm. Always hold your baby securely. Note: Gas tablets or medicines should not be the first choice.
Eh	"I need to burp." This cry is short and is repeated over and over – "eh, eh, eh." When you hear this sound gently place your baby on your chest with her/his head over your shoulder and gently pat them on the back.

Learn more with the "Dunstan Baby Language" DVD by Priscilla Dunstan (www.dunstanbaby.com).

Suggestions for Responding to a Crying Baby

1. **Feel the baby's cheek or back to see if he/she is feverish.** Check her gums or ears to see if they're red or hot or sore. If she just won't stop crying, call the doctor the next day, or, if an emergency, immediately.

2. **Your baby may have stomach gas or colic caused by a digestive problem.** Gentle movements to relieve pressure on the abdomen are most effective.

3. **Hold your baby, rock him, and relax.** When parents feel stress, babies pick up the stress through their interactions. Hold your baby and gently rock him while you talk to him softly, kiss, hug, and caress him. While you're holding him, take two or three breaths and relax; hug or hum softly. Just because your baby's upset doesn't mean you have to be upset.

4. **Leave your baby for 10-15 minutes if you feel you might hurt her.** This will help you to calm down so you can approach the baby in a more positive frame of mind.

5. **The rhythm of walking back and forth,** while gently bouncing the baby, can put him back to sleep. Telling him all the wonderful things he did that day and how proud you are to be his parent helps you to focus on positive thoughts.

6. **Sing or hum to your baby to calm her or turn the radio** on to something that will be soothing to both of you.

7. **Put the baby in the stroller or car.** The motion can put her back to sleep.

8. **Check the formula.** Your baby may have an allergic reaction to or difficulty digesting cow's milk or prepared formulas; some formulas have too much iron.

9. **Be willing to ask for help from a friend or relative.** Seeking help is a sign of health and critical in maintaining positive mental health.

10. **Take time to rest or sleep while your baby sleeps.** Your baby is not crying to be mean-spirited; she is just being a baby!

Responding to Children Exploring Danger

Your baby's increased mobility through crawling expands his ability to learn from his environment. All areas of the home become opportunities for learning. No areas are taboo, including kitchen cleansers, sharp knives, hot ovens, electric sockets, or climbing on high objects. Yelling at your child, threatening her, making statements of doom, telling her what not to do, physically jerking her away, spanking or slapping her for touching a dangerous object or entering an area unassisted are all inappropriate responses. These only reflect that **you** are dangerous.

Suggestions for Responding to a Child's Exploration

1. **Baby-proof the house.** Create an environment where your children can enjoy playing safely.

2. **Adopt a non-hitting attitude.** Replace feelings of violence with feelings of caring.

3. **Use verbal and physical redirection as a means of managing your child's behavior.** In a firm voice, let the child know he is performing or about to perform an unacceptable behavior. Approach the child, stoop down, make eye contact, and gently hold his hands. Tell the child his behavior is unacceptable. Attempt to let the child reestablish the original setting - returning an object; turning off an appliance; being gentle with an object or animal. Use nurturing touch and verbal statements to redirect the child to perform more appropriate behavior. Take a dangerous object away and substitute a safer one, such as large plastic bowls, puzzles, coloring or scribbling on paper. Engage the child in play; e.g., a tent made with a blanket. Praise the child for cooperating, and being a good listener. "Praise for doing" will reinforce future encounters. Repeat above if necessary.

Responding to Very Active Children

When your two-year old runs noisily around the house, perhaps blocking your view of or interrupting your ability to listen to the TV or radio, it is important to have realistic expectations of his/her capabilities, given his/her age and level of development. Many children under five or six do not have a clear concept of spatial relationships, and they may not know when they are standing in someone's line of view. They may not comprehend your inability to listen to a TV or radio program. Children of this age usually have a high activity level and need plenty of exercise.

Suggestions for Responding to Very Active Children

1. Instead of encouraging the attention-seeking part of the child's behavior, think before you act in yelling, threatening, or putting down.

2. Talk to your spouse or to another parent in order to understand your child.

3. Think about the causes of your child's behavior.

4. Enjoy your child's energy level, and let him/her know it.

5. Redirect your child to a calmer activity.

6. Combine your need and your child's need.

7. Postpone your own activity or record the TV program for later viewing.

8. Sometimes, choose to satisfy your child's need rather than your own.

9. If your child is in danger (e.g., running into the street or reaching for a hot pot on the stove), you may find yourself yelling to get his attention and prevent him from being hurt. Even here, however, you can think after you act and prevent the problem from occurring again.

Responding to Children's Oppositional Behavior

When your request is followed by your child's refusal, asking again, pleading, giving her choices when you really don't mean to, demanding, and finally blowing up and making threats that both you and your child know are exaggerated, as you both reach a standoff are inappropriate responses.

Suggestions for Responding to Oppositional Behavior

1. Say what you really want; don't give choices when there aren't any.

2. Give the child transition time to disengage from one activity and reengage in a new activity. The younger the child, the more critical the transition time.

3. Build your child's self-esteem. A happy child who perceives herself as competent and capable is a much easier child to direct, encourage, and manage.

4. Use your sense of humor to exaggerate the situation, brighten up a dreary situation, or use reverse psychology to accomplish a task.

5. Role-playing is effective in delivering of choices and messages. Brainstorm ways to enhance a child's self-esteem.

6. Nightly, tell your children empowering stories that recap only the day's events that were positive, productive, cooperative, well-meaning, and meaningful.

7. Praise your children for cooperating and for who they are.

8. Take time to laugh with your children every day. And you do not need a reason to engage in laughter! Laughter is good for both of you.

Responding When Children Get Angry

Like adults, young children experience a wide range of emotions, including anger. Their anger often comes from frustration when they attempt something that is difficult. Other reasons young children get angry include hunger, fatigue, or an insistence on doing things their own way. Angry children can be a challenge to deal with, especially when parents respond by getting angry themselves – then children learn by example. The problem is that yelling and threatening create an atmosphere of fear, rather than one of understanding, love, and trust. Furthermore, when parents yell and threaten, they do not teach children how to deal with their own anger.

Suggestions for Responding to a Child's Anger

1. Recognize when your child's frustration is rising and intervene before things start flying.

2. When promoting family rules, emphasize the "do" rules rather than the "don't" rules.

3. Acknowledge and manage your own anger.

4. Model the desired behavior: stay calm, help your child, and talk him through the activity.

5. Empathize with your child, and let her know you understand her feelings.

6. Keep a sense of humor.

7. Encourage your child to express his feelings in creative artwork and listen to his response. Little boys are more likely to communicate their feelings while involved in an activity.

8. Redirect your child to a less frustrating activity.

9. Remind your child firmly and calmly of the rules. Give her a choice that is logically related to the behavior. Follow through. Do not get into power struggles over every little thing. Have fun together and show your child you love her.

Meeting Children's Needs When Parents Are Busy

Parents often find that they are busy and preoccupied simultaneously when their children desire attention. If parents have not set down some priorities, these can be stressful times. Getting angry, yelling, or moving toward your child menacingly are inappropriate responses.

Suggestions for Responding to Children's Needs During Busy Times

1. **Establish clear family rules.** Around two years of age children will begin to understand the idea of rules. Consistent guidelines help everyone know what is expected and to take responsibility for their own behavior. Remember family rules are for everyone in the family, not just for children. Generally, children three years of age and older are capable of following family rules. The seven easy steps to follow when establishing rules for your family are:
    • Get everyone to participate.
    • Share with everyone problem behaviors that are unacceptable.

- Brainstorm with everyone a short list of rules.
- Keep the rules simple.
- Identify a punishment and reward for each rule.
- Limit the family rules to a maximum of five.
- Drop and add new rules to the list when needed, or as others become automatic.
- When new problem behaviors appear, have a family meeting and repeat the above steps.

2. **Communicate with your children often.** Listen to their opinion, thoughts, ideas, and feelings without being critical and condemning.

3. **Model the desired behavior, inviting your children to be involved in the "game" of life.** Remember that children often mirror the behavior of their parents; make certain that your behavior is appropriate and could be videotaped for public showing.

Responding to Whining Children

Supermarkets, toy stores, etc. are very tempting to children. Unless clear expectations are established in advance, it is very possible that children will ask for, whine, and demand things. Aggravating as a child's whining may be, threats and put-downs are unlikely to solve the problem. Specifically, threats intimidate children, without teaching them an alternative to whining, and sometimes parents make threats that are dangerous, such as leaving a child alone in a store. Put-downs are destructive for several reasons: they teach the child that put-downs are acceptable; they are global statements about the child's character; and they create an atmosphere of disrespect rather than love.

Suggestions for Responding to Whining Children

1. Have a family meeting, discuss the issue, and agree to one set of rules.
2. Calmly and clearly communicate expectations to your child in advance.
3. Help your child practice the desired behavior ahead of time.
4. Give your child a snack before entering a supermarket.
5. Give your child a job to do in the store and praise him when he is helpful.
6. Be firm: do not encourage whining with weak statements or by whining yourself.
7. Consider rewarding your child at the end of the shopping trip if she has acted appropriately.
8. Follow through firmly and calmly with the rules and expectations you have established.

Responding to Fighting Siblings

Sibling conflict is common and often distressing to parents. It can disrupt the home environment, and sometimes be a symptom of problems at home, at school, or in the neighborhood. Even so, when handled constructively, sibling conflict can provide opportunities for children to learn healthy, non-violent ways to settle conflict. It will help parents if they understand why siblings fight:

1. **They may have a legitimate difference and not know how to resolve it peacefully.** They may want attention from their parents or compete for their parents' love.

2. **They may be taking out on each other something else that is bothering them.** They may fight because they are at different developmental levels and their abilities or needs clash. They may imitate the behavior of adults or older children. They may be bored and getting on each other's nerves.

Suggestions for Responding to Fighting Siblings

1. **Hold a family meeting.** Take turns listening and talking, using "I" and "feelings" statements. As a parent, acknowledge any part you may have in a pattern of family fighting.

2. **Agree on rules for peacefully solving disagreements.** Be specific about behaviors that are desirable. Write the rules and post them so they are easy to see.

3. **Set a positive example** of peaceful conflict resolution.

4. **Learn to distinguish between different levels of conflict.** If it is a minor disagreement, ignore it and let the children work it out while you observe.

5. **Stop the fighting and remove the object of disagreement.** If it is squabbling that could get out of control, with name-calling, hitting, kicking, etc., you need to intervene.

6. **Separate the children.** If it is fighting that is already out of control, with abusive language or violence, remind them that insults and physical attacks are not allowed. Have them go to separate areas to cool off.

7. **Help the children learn to problem-solve without violence.** Explain that they need to use appropriate language, listen without interrupting, and reach a solution acceptable to everyone concerned. Demonstrate by example and give them an opportunity to practice their problem-'solving skills.

8. **If the children have difficulty solving the problem, help them.** Your goal should be to help them learn to settle it themselves. Do not impose your own solution unless they absolutely cannot reach a settlement. Listen to their ideas. Suggest a few of your own. Write the ideas down.

9. **Have patience** and remain impartial and fair.

Children in the Middle-School Age Group

Children in this age group are undergoing a huge period of adjustment, from their rapidly changing bodies to an entirely new social structure. They have not grown this rapidly since they were two years old. But don't worry; all of their adolescent craziness should subside soon…around the end of high school!

Physical Changes in Boys and Girls

Girls grow 3.3 inches per year during the peak of puberty and boys up to 3.7 inches annually. Girls sometimes tower over boys at this age because puberty typically starts earlier for girls, around ages 9 to 13; for boys, ages 10 to 16. Girls' arms, legs and feet might be growing faster than the rest of the body. The school nurse may start scoliosis checks – curvature of the spine, commonly associated with early-adolescent growth spurts. Acne breakouts will begin because of high hormone levels, which increase oil and sweat production – use astringent and antiperspirant.

Because of the impulsiveness and egocentrism that can come now, they're not always tactful about telling you how stupid you are.

Girls Only: Girls begin developing a woman's shape, with wider hips and smaller waist. Fat will build up in the abdomen, buttocks, and legs; girls can gain as much as 20-25 pounds. Girls sometimes react negatively to the weight gain and develop eating disorders. Weight gain is perfectly natural; it's the body's way of preparing for reproduction. This leads to bras for girls as young as 6-7 and, later, razors for shaving armpits and legs. Between ages 9-16 girls begin menstruation. You need to begin the conversation about sex.

Boys Only: The level of testosterone increases and a ten- or voice may drop to a bass, with some cracking along the way. Muscles begin to enlarge. Consult with a doctor about a safe time to start weight-training. It may also be the time to discuss the dangers of steroids. They will start to sprout hair everywhere. Sperm production begins and sexual organs grow. You need to begin the conversation about sex.

Mental Changes in Boys and Girls

With the rapid development of their bodies, boys and girls also have an influx of hormones. Their brains are developing new faculties that come with increased responsibilities. The frontal cortex, most related to planning, decision-making, impulse and self-control, is still under construction during this stage of adolescence. Gray matter grows more than the brain can sustain, so a "pruning" process begins, allowing cells and connections that are not used to wither and die. Boys and girls begin to develop interests in things such as art, math, music, or sports. They begin to think broadly and abstractly, gaining the ability to hypothesize about possibilities they never saw before. But it's a work in progress. During early adolescence, a new egocentrism emerges; they become more self-conscious and concerned about how they're viewed by others. Keep in mind that your child's relationship with you, the parent, can keep them from giving in to negative influences; the stronger the relationship, the stronger his/her ability to resist peer pressure. But, de-idealizing of mom and/or dad may also be taking place; it's one of the ways your child begins to see him/herself as an individual. And because of the impulsiveness and egocentrism that can come now, they're not always tactful about telling you how stupid you are.

A Homeless Child's Right to Attend School

A child is homeless if she does not have a permanent home – that is, a fixed, regular, and adequate place to stay at night. This includes a child living in many different places under many different circumstances. It includes a child who is living with a friend or relative because the family lost its home or cannot afford housing. It includes a child who is living in a motel, hotel, trailer park, camping grounds, or a space not usually used as a residence, such as a car or abandoned building. A child may also be homeless if he is a runaway or a child who has been kicked out by his parents. It also includes a child who is awaiting foster care placement.

A homeless child is entitled to the same free public education available to all.

A homeless child is entitled to the same free public education available to all other students. In addition, as long as a child is homeless, she can stay in the same school if that is what is best for her. School may be the only thing in her life that provides stability to an unstable situation. Furthermore, homeless children can do as well as other children; some have been known to go from homeless to Harvard or Stanford University! These children overcame despair and found meaning by what they did, what they experienced, and how they handled the unmanageable, tragic situations in life.

Attention-Deficit/Hyperactivity Disorder and Hope

A diagnosis of ADHD presents both a challenge and an opportunity for parents. The primary challenge is to see ADHD as the problem, not your child, yourself, or your family as a source of blame. And perhaps you may then be able to experience your child's ADHD as an opportunity to effectively channel the creativity and enthusiasm that often accompany this disorder. (Note: For information about ADHD, suggestions and laws protecting your child, search the Internet site www.ADHDSupportCompany.com.)

A child with ADHD is not like other children. The set of rules and expectations that governs most children does not apply when dealing with ADHD children. Cultivating your often bright and creative child is well worth the extra effort it takes to see that his more demanding needs for a nurturing environment are met. ADHD is often an inherited condition. **The three types of ADHD are inattentive, hyperactive-impulsive, and combined.** Some effects of untreated ADHD in children include lower-than-expected grades, difficulty taking tests, poor organizational and study skills, failing a grade, and difficulty making and keeping friends. Untreated children become untreated adolescents who engage in risk-taking behavior that can lead to major legal, financial, emotional, academic, and substance abuse problems. By adulthood, many may experience career underachievement and job instability. A three-tiered management approach for ADHD is often recommended, including behavioral therapy, education, and medication.

ADHD is diagnosed less often in girls, perhaps because the symptoms are somewhat different from those in boys. Girls with ADHD often display anxiety, depression, and learning or cognitive problems. Boys with ADHD may act in a very angry, rebellious fashion. Girls may withdraw and become depressed if they feel overwhelmed and socially rejected at school. Highly hyperactive-impulsive girls may engage in constant dramatic screaming battles at home. Helping them to reestablish emotional equilibrium, especially in relation to hormonal fluctuations, is critical. Teach your daughter to establish a "quiet zone" in her life. Try to minimize corrections and criticism. Help her look for ways in which to excel. And seek medical treatment if your daughter's premenstrual syndrome (PMS) symptoms are severe.

At school, suggest that your child sit near the teacher and the chalkboard to help him pay attention better. Suggest that he sit near students who do their work and do not fool around or talk too much. Suggest that he sit away from distractions. Your child should use an assignment notebook and write down every assignment as soon as the teacher gives it. Ask the teacher to let you know on Friday which assignments were not passed on. Help your child keep his/her backpack cleaned out and organized. Suggest that your child keep all assignments in her folders, to check the folder for every subject, and to make sure to turn them in. Suggest that your child work with her teacher or counselor to help learn good study skills, test-taking skills, organizational skills, and time-management skills. Ask that your child's teacher fill out a daily or weekly progress report so that he/she does not fall behind.

When Your Child Misbehaves
1. Identify the problem. Be specific. **Do not** label your child with the problem, e.g., substituting the problem of a messy bedroom with, "You are a messy, messy child."
2. Identify what you have already tried.
3. Identify the behavior you want to see instead.
4. Brainstorm ways to achieve the desired behavior.
5. Try new ideas. Be willing to reassess the problem and ask for help.

Signs of Behaviors That Mirror Family Problems
1. Increasing rebelliousness.
2. Increasing destructiveness.
3. Drugs and alcohol are replacing other pleasures in life.
4. Stealing has replaced work in obtaining 'wants'.
5. Increasing aggressiveness and acting out as the child ages: first towards

inanimate objects; then, animate objects such as pets; then, siblings; then, peers; finally, towards those with whom he/she has a relationship.

6. Increasing fantasies of wanting to do harm to the abuser.

7. Decreasing ability to deal with or express feelings.

8. Increased display of negative behaviors in order to be the center of attention.

Using Negotiation and Compromise to Resolve an Impasse

1. Determine if there is a difference of opinion between you and another person.

2. State your views and the views of the other person(s).

3. Check if your impression of the problem and your understanding of their views are accurate.

4. Offer a compromise. The other person will either accept or reject your offer.

5. Keep negotiating until both parties have reached a mutual acceptance.

Children and Teens as Copycats

When children have become, or are becoming, disciplinary problems, after you have read how-to-books, looked into 'tough love' courses and various types of 'parent effectiveness' training, you might want to examine your own behavior and how it might be affecting your children. Parents are role models for their children. But often they fail to make the connection between their actions and those of their children. Consider the following examples.

1. **Recreational Use**. A mother buys marijuana for her teenage daughter and her friends and smokes it with them, calling it recreational use. Why is the mother shocked when her daughter later becomes addicted to cocaine that began as "recreational"?

2. **Like Father, Like Son.** A husband abruptly leaves his wife and moves in with another woman. His two sons never say much, but both become sexually active early in high school and defiant when their parents object. The father's dismay is understandable, but why is he surprised when the older boy tells him that he is in no position to moralize? Later one of the sons becomes infected with hepatitis B or HIV.

3. **Family Communications.** A dad whose temperamental outburst regularly unsettles his family hears his son bad-mouthing a referee who made a call the boy didn't like.

4. **A Family Affair**. A mother who has had numerous affairs and several marriages is distraught because her 16-year-old daughter dresses provocatively and gets picked up at the airport by a middle-aged man who buys her expensive gifts. The daughter can't understand why her mother is making such a big deal about it.

This is not to suggest that parents are always to blame for their children's misbehavior. There are, of course, many things that shape the growing child: temperament, constitution, intelligence, peers, and culture. But **what parents do is at least as important as what they tell their children to do.** And parents are less likely to recognize, let alone admit, the significance of their behavior.

Human beings are adept at all kinds of avoidance – they deny, externalize, rationalize, project, and ignore. **It is hard for us to admit that we make choices,** and that we are responsible for those choices. Maybe this is why we're having difficulty disciplining our children. We aren't doing a good job of disciplining ourselves. And when we don't do a good job of disciplining ourselves, consider the fact that the odds of a child going to prison when that child has a recidivist parent, one who repeatedly returns to prison, are 92 to one! On the other hand, some children who object to poor choices made by parents seize the opportunity to live completely differently, including how they raise their own children.

Discipline is half of the story. **Kids detect hypocrisy.** We're not implying that parents need to be unfailing models of moral rectitude. Children are very forgiving of their parents when the bond is a strong one. But many children spend a great deal of time alone and unsupervised. Some parents feel that presents, phone calls, cards, and letters can make up for their absence. **But children need the time, attention, unconditional love, and presence that only their parents can provide, not presents**. Therapy will not suffice. Neglected children embody the term 'failure to thrive' as much as any malnourished child in the Third World. Sometimes, at least one or both parents must make major lifestyle changes. The choice is yours.

Thirteen Factors for a Healthy, Win/Win Family

1. Willingness to speak and listen thoughtfully to one another.
2. Ability to bring quarrels to a quick and satisfying conclusion without bearing grudges.
3. Cooperation among family members in helping each other maintain a secure and positive self-image.
4. Atmosphere of frequent playfulness and humor but without sarcasm or put-downs.
5. Clear parental guidelines on right and wrong. Treat problems without labeling the offender.
6. System of sharing responsibility.
7. Creation of strong sense of unity and respect for family traditions and rituals.
8. Easy interaction among all family members. Everyone is encouraged to participate in activities, and creation of factions is discouraged.
9. Sharing of some common spiritual or ethical core though not necessarily tied to an established church or denomination.
10. Respect for one another's privacy.
11. Development of a spirit of volunteerism and community service beyond the family's immediate needs.

12. Desire to share some leisure time, but not all of the time.

13. Willingness, when serious problems cannot be solved, to go outside the family for help.

Family Law Facilitators

The Office of the Family Law Facilitator is located in every county and provides self-represented parties with necessary information, forms, and procedures related to child support, spousal support, and health insurance issues. If you become incarcerated and are responsible for child support, you should contact the D.A. in your county immediately. Do not wait until you are eventually released.

A Family Law Facilitator is an attorney licensed to practice law in your state, who has been appointed by a superior court of a state county. Each superior court is required to maintain an Office of the Family Law Facilitator to assist self-represented persons regardless of their income, with issues of child support, spousal support, and health insurance.

The family law facilitator can help you with child support, spousal support, and health insurance issues, and can:

- Give you educational materials.
- Give you court forms.
- Assist you with court forms.
- Calculate guideline child support.
- Refer you to the local child support agency (LCSA), family court services, and other community agencies.

The family law facilitator cannot represent you or the other party. He is a neutral person. Both you and the other party in your case may receive assistance from the same family law facilitator. There is no attorney-client privilege between the family law facilitator and any person he or she assists. Matters discussed with the family law facilitator are not confidential. The family law facilitator is not responsible for the outcome of your case.

For specific or strategic legal advice in your case, contact a private attorney or the bar association's lawyer referral service to ask for a short consultation at a low cost.

You'll need to take the following documents with you when you visit or contact the family law facilitator:

- All relevant court documents
- Your last three paycheck stubs
- Proof of other income (i.e., rental income, tips, Social Security, unemployment, workers compensation, disability, or other money received)
- A copy of your most recent federal and state tax returns

If you need copies of your court file, go to the court clerk's office where your case is filed to obtain copies. There is a fee for copies unless you qualify for a fee waiver. Ask the court clerk for the fee waiver form.

Assistance with an out-of-county case: In the case of California, a family law facilitator in any county can provide you with basic forms, information, and procedures related to child support issues. However, the family law facilitator in the county where the action is filed is best equipped to assist you with questions on local procedures and case information.

Foreign-language interpreters: Some family law facilitator offices may have bilingual staff that can assist when available, but if you need an interpreter it is best to bring your own.

For a referral to a Family Law Facilitator search on the website www.ncsc.org/top ics/children-families-and-elders/family-courts/state-links.aspx.

Organizations for Parents

1. **American Mothers Inc.:** P. O. Box 400, Pound Ridge, NY 10576 (877/242-4264)

2. **Families First:** 2005 Baynard Blvd, Wilmington, DE 19802 (302/658-5177)

3. **Families Working Together:** 5728 West Blvd, Los Angeles, CA 90043 (323-292-7684)

4. **Fathers/Men's Rights Center:** 4195 E Thousand Oaks Blvd, #201, Thousand Oaks, CA 91362 (805-497-1400)

5. **Fathers' Rights:** 3401 Katella Ave, Los Alamitos, CA 90720 (562-493-6064)

6. **Fathers' Rights Center:** 777 W Vista Way, Vista, CA 92083 (760-758-8399)

7. **National Congress for Fathers and Children:** 9454 Wilshire, Suite 207, Beverly Hills, CA 90212 (310-247-6051)

8. **Women Against Gun Violence:** 8800 Venice Blvd, Los Angeles, CA 90034 (310-204-2348)

9. **Women Against Rape:** 2321 Coddington Ctr, Santa Rosa, CA 95401 (707-545-7273)

10. **Women Alive:** 1566 S Burnside Ave, Los Angeles, CA 90019 (323-965-1564)

11. **Women and Children Nutrition:** 4555 E 3rd St, #1D, Los Angeles, CA 90022 (323-262-1136)

12. **Women and Families Commission:** 1160 State Office Bldg, Salt Lake City, UT 84114 (801-538-1736)

13. **Women Helping Women Inc.:** 543 N Fairfax Ave, Los Angeles, CA 90036 (323-655-3807)

14. **Women Infants Children Program:** 1250 Sutterville Rd, Sacramento, CA 95822 (916-737-3677)

15. **Women's International League:** 4603 Prospect Ave, Los Angeles, CA 90027 (213-891-4517)

16. **Legal Services for Prisoners with Children:** 1540 Market St, Suite 490, San Francisco 94102. Request a copy of *A Manual for Incarcerated Parents: Your Legal Rights and Responsibilities*

"Research has shown that children with parents in prison are more likely to exhibit low self-esteem, depression, emotional withdrawal, and inappropriate or disruptive behavior in school. They are 'invisible,' meaning few know their family circumstances. Some studies have shown that children of incarcerated parents are at a higher risk of becoming delinquent or engaging in criminal behavior. These impacts are linked to the larger effect of incarceration on the family, which can include the lost of financial and emotional support as well as the social stigma of having a family member imprisoned, and the loss of child care which enables other family members to work."

– "From Prison to Home" Conference. January 30-31, 2002.

Background paper. Washington, DC: Urban Institute.

Chapter 8

Positive Relationships, Marriage, and Love

We are the children of our parents,
For brother and sister, what are we?
Whose face we have never seen.

We are the children of our parents,
Whose voice we have never heard.

We are the children of our parents,
To whom we cried for strength and
Comfort in our agony and pain.

We are the children of our parents,
Whose lives, like ours, were lived in
Solitude in the wilderness.

We are the children of our parents,
To whom only we can speak out the
Strange dark burden of our heart
and spirit.

We are the children of our parents,
And we shall follow the
Prints of their feet forever
Until we decide to make responsible
and meaningful choices.

– a parody of a poem by Thomas Wolfe

Importance of Relationships

All human beings crave for and certainly need social contacts. Relationships are very important to humans, whatever age, whatever nationality, whichever sex. Without relationships, life is empty, boring and lonely. With, relationships, lives are fun, fulfilling and sometimes stressful. Relationships are rewarding, but a struggle too. Relationships are particularly important to your success in transitioning from prison, to parole, and to life after discharge.

Relationships however, change and develop over time. For example, relationships with parents change, moving towards more equality as we grow and become more independent. We start to develop interests outside the family and build closer relationships with our peers.

Relationships vary between different people and different groups. Those who are in positions of authority expect us to obey them, and we expect them to know what they are talking about, so typically we do as they say. Friends expect us to offer support, encouragement and fun, which is what we expect from them. And we need to develop skills if we are to maintain happy, healthy and rewarding relationships.

The pace of life today is such that often relationships are given a low priority in our list of things to be attended to. It is important is that your relationships are built on strong ground. A strong social support will play an important role in helping you lead a healthy stress-free life. Relationship is a feeling or sense of emotional bonding with another.

Our relationships are also a fundamental source of learning. The quality of the relationship deeply influences the hopefulness required to remain curious and open to new experiences, and the capacity to see connections and discover meanings. We feel "related" when we feel at one with another (person or object) in some heartfelt way.

Communication within relationships is also an important factor. If we do not communicate well, the relationship will suffer. We can discuss issues, raise conflicts (assertively, not aggressively), negotiate and make decisions. A relationship is a medium through which we are allowed to flourish. It involves an emotional connection with others and can animate us. Hence, it is important to take a good deep look at the relationships in the life you are about to enter. Pay a little more attention to nurturing relationships which allow you to grow as strong as the effort you put into it.

This chapter will present basic differences between men and women, and their relationships. It also discusses personalities and behaviors that are constructive or destructive. When you fill your life with meaningful activities, meaningful relationships will seek you out

Men and Women *are* From Earth

Men and women are uniquely different and thus irreplaceable. Mutual respect and love facilitates the mutual self-transcendence of both partners, opening up a new world of values in an upward spiral of growth. Good relationships bring out the best in each other; bad relationships bring out the worst. Many relationships experience difficulty because they are rooted in a disordered philosophy focused on individual self-realization rather than as a committed whole that complements each other in actualizing marital values. Faithfulness ensues as the reflection of each partner's commitment. Developing a positive relationship in any friendship, partnership, or marriage is an art that must be practiced.

Actions or Behaviors That Result in Negative Relationships

1. **Co-dependency:** To be overly involved with another person(s) to the point that your health and stability are jeopardized. To feel both reactive to and overly responsible for the other person's feelings and behavior.
2. **Contemptuous:** To openly disrespect another based on differences in life experiences.
3. **Controlling:** To dominate, breeding hostility, fear, and alienation.
4. **Critical:** To find fault and to be judgmental of another person.
5. **Defensiveness:** To justify negative behaviors.
6. **Domination:** To attempt to rule by superior authority or power.
7. **Lack of Affection/Lack of Respect:** When these are absent, the relationship probably cannot be saved.
8. **Manipulation:** To influence shrewdly or deviously.
9. **Neglectful:** To disregard, ignore, pay partial or no attention to. Neglect is the leading cause of failed relationships and the problem that men tend to recognize the least. Very few women divorce because of physical abuse, infidelity, alcoholism, criminal behavior, fraud, or other serious grounds. Quite simply, women usually leave men because they are neglected.

10. **To Scapegoat:** To blame other person(s) for problems.

11. **Separatism:** To choose to spend more time apart rather than face issues.

12. **Withdrawal:** To remove oneself physically, emotionally, and socially.

Character Disorders Contributing to Negative Relationships

Toxic personalities can poison your life. Such people have psychological conditions where certain character traits are exaggerated and interfere with relationships. Usually such people lack insight into their thinking and are inflexible when they have to deal with a crisis. The passive-aggressive, obsessive-compulsive, and the narcissist are three of the most troublesome personality types and can create tremendous relationship problems. A better understanding of how others think and act can enable you to create a win-win scenario.

- **Passive-aggressive:** Frustrates a relationship with covert hostility, sneaky insults, and calculated inefficiency. This personality may be the most difficult to deal with. This person is negative and obstructionist. Nothing that anyone else says or does is good. He is also moody. He likes to see other people miserable, and gets pleasure from seeing someone else squirm. He will push buttons to see how fast you react. Often he is unreasonable and demanding. **Coping Strategies:** First, as difficult as this may be, try to make an ally of this person. Keep your cool. Don't let him see you get angry. That's what the person wants. Reward him for behaving well. Give praise when appropriate. Walk out of the room if it's a no-win situation. Look for an alternative to solving the problem.

- **Hysteric:** Over-dramatizes problems and makes minor ones into major ones. Acts as a victim. **Coping Strategies:** Do not buy into the drama. Reward her each time she takes responsibility for her life.

- **Narcissist:** Tends to be in love with self. Wants the benefits of the relationship without having to work at it. He or she is manipulative and feels inferior. At the same time, he is often arrogant and feels he is special and that others should treat him as being special. He thinks he knows it all. **Coping Strategies:** First, don't expect to change these individuals. You will be wasting time and effort. Second, set boundaries and limits. Narcissists are famous for dumping work on others while they sit back and take the credit. You can learn a lot from the narcissist in terms of how to handle others with confidence and style.

- **Sociopath:** Is the irresponsible charmer who seems to be without a conscience. Cons friends, partners, or significant other. **Coping Strategies:** Set boundaries and limits. Learn to recognize the difference between those who give without any expectations and those who don't. Also, practice saying "No" until you feel comfortable.

- **Obsessive-compulsive:** Tends to be caught up in minute details. Loses sight of the overall picture and the main tasks that need to be done. Her thinking is in black-and-white terms. Has few people skills and is very critical of everyone and everything. **Coping Strategies:** First, don't get caught up in the perfectionist game. Just do your best. Also, don't beat up on yourself if you are not living up to the obsessive-compulsive standards. Remember that even if she is a perfectionist, you don't have to be.

Actions or Behaviors That Result in Positive Relationships

1. Recognize the commonality as well as the inherent differences between each other. To seek to know all each others likes and dislikes. To cherish and embrace your differences.
2. Create a relationship and vital community that supports the unique values of each other.
3. Work together without attempting to control each other.
4. Reconnect with truth, that is, "We love each other and we accept our differences."
5. Have positive regard, affection, and respect for each other.
6. Actively seek to understand each other and be present in each other's life.
7. Conspicuously take time out to turn 'toward' one another.
8. Reserve some time and space for yourself each day to relax and give thanks in all things.
9. Consciously seek to be present in each other's lives.
10. Share positive and cheerful communication with each other.
11. Make an effort to compliment each other daily – verbally, in writing, and other ways.
12. Praise to others about your significant other, friends, and children within their earshot.
13. Strive to be compassionate, interdependent, and cooperative.
14. Communicate your warm feelings with a simple touch, caress, and hug.
15. Find time to have fun and laughter each day with each other.
16. Listen intently without any outside sensory chatter and to reflect/paraphrase back what you understood.
17. Finally, say, "I love you" daily, even if it's 500 times! Say it, write it, or communicate it in other ways – with hugs for example. This is especially important in your relationship with your children.

Basic Techniques for Long-lasting Relationships

1. Good, clear communications are basic, as are the willingness to work through arguments, fights, other disagreements.
2. Continue to treat your partner like your best friend.
3. Hold your marriage primary even if it means saying "no" to worthy persons and causes occasionally.
4. Have fun and laugh together often.
5. Remember that a loving relationship grows, develops, changes, and evolves.

6. Make time for each other, and just each other, for emotional and spiritual renewal.

7. A loving relationship ultimately transcends everything we know about it.

Keys to Preserving Marriage

- **Spiritual qualities:** Sensitivity to others includes empathy, feeling the pain of another, and sharing in their joys.

- **Gratitude and appreciation:** Instead of focusing on what you don't have, focus on what you have.

- **Resilience:** Life has disappointments. You can succumb to hopelessness and despair, or push forward and break out and triumph. Examples: Michael Fox, Lance Armstrong, Senator Max Cleland, Christopher Reeve, Stephen Hawking, and many other well-known persons.

- **Anger transformed:** Fear directed outward as an idolatrous impulse can be destructive on self and others if not transformed creatively, socially, spiritually, or existentially in a positive direction.

- **Meaning:** A sense of transcendent purpose and meaning is as essential to life as food and drink. Without it, we sink into aimlessness, boredom, and despair. "When there is a why, a person can bear almost any what."(Friedrich Nietzche)

- **Working at a relationship:** In order to form a successful relationship, we must first endeavor to be a successful person. Too often, in a relationship we expect the other person to complete us. Unfortunately, the dynamics are such that we must try to be a good person first, so we can bring our best selves into the relationship. Then the alliance becomes greater than the sum of its parts. Marriage does not make a bad person good; it can make a good person better. It takes a lot of introspection, study, and spiritual growth. Part of the problem in relationships lies in the fact that we don't invest time and energy with our significant other to make it work. The average amount of time spouses spend in meaningful communication is less than 20 minutes a week. We are not sharing, communicating, or aspiring enough. Yet there's nothing more important to life than one's relationship(s). Nobody on his deathbed ever, said "I wish that I had spent more time at the office."

- **Misplaced priorities:** We often allow trivia or negativity of life to consume our attention and energies. At the end of our life we see the opportunities we've missed. The tragedy is that we failed to take advantage of all the good we could have done.

- **Learning to be a giver, not a taker:** We often enter a relationship or a marriage unwilling to commit ourselves to work at it. We are so preoccupied with daily activities, so preoccupied with our jobs, so worn down by our external commitments that we don't have the energy to work at a relationship; we just want it to happen by itself. We expect it to grow and deepen and be a source of comfort without putting work into it. We measure the values of a relationship by how many of our desires are met.

A sage sees a boy eating fish with gusto, saying, "I love fish!" so the sage asks the boy, "If you really love fish, why are you eating it? Shouldn't you be feeding it and ensuring that it is comfortable?" When we talk about "loving" someone we are often really referring to how it gratifies us personally. Such love is selfish, not selfless. It is not a love of giving, not a love of nurturing, but a love of selfish gratification. When the "love" we bring to a marriage is no deeper than the "love" that a boy has for a fish, then our marriage is in trouble.

In some cultures the word for love is contained in the term "work." It doesn't just mean I will earn money; it means I will work to love. Romantic passion is mostly gratification of our physical needs, but this love is a conscious effort to give of ourself to someone else. That love does not come instinctively. It takes development, time, and commitment. The true love of a marriage is not the love that precedes the marriage, but the love after marriage that results from giving and sharing and working things out **together**. To paraphrase John F. Kennedy: "Ask not what your marriage can do for you, but what you can do for your marriage." The paradox of marriage is that as we become less concerned with the satisfaction of our needs, we will find that more of our needs are being met. When our spouse feels that he or she is genuinely being cared for, they will go out of their way to care for us.

Finally, remember that no two marriages are alike and none are perfect, but each can improve. In the words of the mother of NBA power forward, Tim Duncan: "Good, better, best; never let it rest until your good is better and your better is best."

Keys to Active Listening in a Marriage

Do's

- Turn off all outside distractions (TV, radio, stereo).
- Remove all reading material from immediate area.
- Select a private area out of sight and sound of other family members.
- Maintain eye contact.
- Look interested.
- Be interested.
- Attempt to remember what you are being told.
- Listen for what is not said as well as what is said.
- Attempt to paraphrase back, in your own words, what you heard.
- Ask questions only to clarify what your spouse is saying and to draw him or her out.

Don'ts

- Interrupt.
- Give advice.
- Criticize.
- Be contemptuous.
- Stare off into space.
- Tell the story of another's similar experience.
- Judge.
- Express opinions.
- Attempt to solve a problem when no request was made.

Rules for Constructive Quarreling

1. Quarrel about only one thing at a time.
2. "Hit-and-run" quarreling must not be allowed.
3. Keep your voice down.
4. Keep to the truth, the problem, without labeling each other.
5. Don't make "you" accusations. Instead, make "I" statements.
6. Say what's upsetting you. Don't be silent about it just to keep the peace.
7. Call for "time out" if emotions are getting too hurt or the argument is getting too hot for intelligent arguing.
8. After each has listened to what the other has to say, trade places verbally.
9. Don't punctuate your words with door slamming or other displays of anger.
10. Don't retaliate. It leads to an escalation of hostilities.
11. Adopt a no-fault attitude to problems.
12. Don't blast the other person with threats and catastrophes.
13. Never bring anyone else into the argument.
14. Never argue in sight or sound of children.

Time Out: An Exercise in Love

You and your partner may disagree on a wide variety of subjects. Sometimes tension builds to the point where violence may erupt. If you feel you are about to become abusive – verbally, physically, or sexually – try taking a time-out instead. In sporting activities, teams use time-outs to regroup and refocus. If they don't, there can be serious consequences in the form of penalties and the narrowing of the playing field. A time-out is not avoiding a conflict or a disagreement. It is temporarily removing yourself from the situation until you have had a chance to calm down and think. Pick a time when you and your partner are not angry to establish the ground rules for using time-out in your relationship.

Agreeing to a Time-out

Either partner can call a time-out. Decide who will stay with the children during the time-out. Agree how you will signal a time-out (Making the "T" sign means "I need to take a time-out.") Agree to acknowledge the time-out when called. Agree no additional talking or touching is to take place once a time-out has been called.

Cues to When to Call a Time-out

When you recognize that you are getting out of control. Your body gets tense or feels like it will explode. You feel yourself getting physically or verbally aggressive. When winning the argument is your sole focus.

Steps to Take When Using a Time-out

State that you are taking a time-out. Don't just leave. Make the "I" statement: "I need a time-out." Leave silently instead of getting in the last word. Do not intrude into each other's space by following the other from room to room, or attempt to keep the other from leaving.

Things to Do When You Take a Timeout

Go for a walk, run or bike ride alone. Concentrate on cooling off. Remember it is possible to physically detach, but remain psychologically engaged, which would result in the time-out being ineffective. Avoid the temptation to go over and over the conflict or to recall past injustices. Work at achieving a perspective that will enable you to empathize – that is, to see the disagreement from your partner's point of view.

Don't drink, use drugs, drive, or divert your anger by becoming involved in any violent sport.

Things to Do After You Are Calm

Consider that you own mistakes (behaviors and thoughts) that contributed to the problem getting out of hand. Recognize that you are partly right and partly wrong, as is your partner. Think about solutions to the issue that are mutually agreeable. Check in with your partner to make sure it is okay to return home.

What to Do Upon Returning Home

Don't insist on immediately resuming the discussion. The signaler should state that he/she was partly right and partly wrong in the preceding conflict, and that he/she is now ready to resume the discussion. If your partner is able to acknowledge that he/she also was not entirely right, then it is safe to continue. If the above does not happen, then a second time-out should be promptly signaled. It is important to realize that a called time-out represents a "success" rather than a failure. Each time a time-out is successfully followed, the level of security and comfort of both partners will increase.

"Time-out" is a very useful tool, but it takes practice. Conscientious effort is the name of the game. For more information to increase effective anger management skill contact a domestic support organization in your county.

A good marriage means falling in love many times, but always with the same person!

Chapter 9

Health for Men, Women, and Children

*Over 75 percent of diseases are diseases of choice.
These diseases spring out of wrong 'loves' that we won't
surrender. They are loves that ultimately lead to
overwhelming stress. The love-addiction to nicotine leads
to the death of over 500,000 people each year in America,
nearly four million each year in China and India.*

HEALTH IS A state of complete physical, mental, spiritual, and social well-being and not merely the absence of disease or infirmity. Wellness begins with a conscious decision to shape a healthy lifestyle maintaining proper diet, weight, physical fitness, and routine medical exams and procedures. It's a mind set, a predisposition to adopt a series of key principles that lead to high levels of well-being and satisfaction. A wellness mind set will protect you against temptations to blame someone else, make excuses, shirk accountability, whine, or wet your pants in the face of adversity.

This chapter examines the secrets of a healthier, happier, and longer life. It outlines the top 10 killing diseases, and lists the recommended immunizations and physical exams for men, women, and children. For more authoritative information on health and wellness, visit these websites:

Centers for Disease Control and Prevention
www.cdc.gov

Cleveland Clinic
www.clevelandclinic.org/health/default.aspx

Mayo Clinic
www.mayoclinic.com/healthinformation/

Medline Plus from the National Institutes of Health
www.nlm.nih.gov/medlineplus/

WebMD.com
www.webmd.com

Secrets for a Healthier, Happier, Longer Life

- **Eat Better to Live Longer.** Limit diet to no more than 30% fat of all kinds. Watch the add-on fat. Add salsa, lemon juice, or fat-free sour cream to pastas, breads, and vegetables that are naturally low in fat. Cut down on meats, especially red meats.

Eat skinless chicken and fish as lower-fat alternatives. Try switching to low-fat or fat-free versions of dairy products. Adopt healthier cooking methods. Steaming, baking, grilling, and microwaving are better than frying. Read the label. Compare the total number of calories to the number of calories of fat (multiply the grams of fat by 9 calories; that is how much each gram contains. If your new number is more than 30% of the total calories, this is a food you want to cut down on.

- **Take Your Vitamins.** A basic daily supplement should give you 100% of vitamins A, B, C, D, E, and K. It should also contain 100% of the RDA for potassium, magnesium, selenium and zinc and at least 100 micrograms of chromium, all of which are needed for a person's good health. An even better supplement is one that's labeled "antioxidant-rich."

- **Get More Fiber** (soluble and insoluble fiber); aim for at least 20 grams per day. Oatmeal, whole-wheat toast, fruit, most vegetables, beans, and other whole-grain breads and pastas help lower your cholesterol level and may help reduce the risk of colon cancer.

- **Don't Diet.** Eat more carbohydrate-rich vegetables, fruits, grains, and legumes. The 10 best fruits and vegetables to eat: apples, blackberries, broccoli, cantaloupe, mangos, oranges, red bell peppers, sweet potatoes, Swiss chard, and tomatoes.

- **Break Free from Stress.** Stress is the top priority health problem facing men and women today. Up to 90% of all visits to doctors are for stress-related and cognitive illnesses. Over 87% of all illnesses are psychosomatic – that is, self-induced. Some of the most successful anti-stress strategies are:

1. 30 minutes of aerobic exercises three or four times each week. Examples: brisk walking, swimming, biking.

2. Hobbies or favorite activities that are completely removed from your business or home activities.

3. Relaxing expectations – expect everything you do to take 20% longer than you think it will.

4. Maintaining a lifestyle that is within your means. Life should not just make us tired. Life should make us happy.

5. Finding the meaning of your life through spiritual involvement, volunteer work, political involvement, listening to classical music, writing, creative endeavors, positive attitude toward experiences and encounters with others, or meditating.

6. Drinking a few glasses of water, stretching, taking deep breaths of air, popping plastic bubbles, laughing for no reason whatsoever, or doing some gentle head rotations.

- **Get in Shape.** 20-45 minutes of aerobic activities daily. Examples: jogging, cycling, brisk walking, stair climbing or swimming. Also, enough resistance weight training to target all the major muscle groups: legs, back, chest, arms, shoulders and abdominal – 3-5 times a week.

Responses to the Top Seven Killing Diseases

- **Heart Disease:** Exercise and follow a healthy diet.

- **Cancer:** Quit smoking. Limit daily alcohol consumption to no more than two drinks. Wear a sunscreen. Reduce fat in your diet to below 30% of total calories. Eat more fruits, vegetables, and fiber.

- **Stroke:** Keep blood pressure down, get your fair share of vitamins, take a baby aspirin regularly (with doctor's approval). Quit smoking and exercise moderately. Eat a banana every day to keep arteries clear. See a doctor for an ECG.

- **Lung Disease:** Quit smoking. Mant people develop or die from lung cancer if they are exposed to tobacco smoke, directly or secondhand.

- **Pneumonia and Influenza:** Get a flu vaccination every year if over age 65. Some people can't because of allergies to eggs. `Get a pneumonia shot after age 60.

- **HIV/HBV/TB:** Practice safe sex religiously. Bank your own blood if facing surgery. Obtain the hepatitis vaccine 3-shot series.

- **Diabetes.** Keep weight down. Lower fat and sugar content of your diet. Exercise regularly. Take antioxidant vitamins.

Recommended Adult Immunization Schedule, by Vaccine and Age Group (updates: www.cdc.gov/vaccines/recs/schedules/default.htm)

- **Tetanus, diphtheria, and pertussis (Td/Tdap):** Ages>19, 1 dose Tdap; 1 dose with Td every 10 years....Influenza: Ages>19, 1 dose annually...Pneumoccoccal: Ages 19-64, 1-2 doses; >65, 1 dose...Zoster: Ages>60, 1 dose.

- **Human Papillomavirus (HPV):** Ages 19-26, 3 doses (females).

- **Measles, mumps, and rubella (MMR):** Ages ≥19, 1 or 2 doses; Ages ≥50, 1 dose if some risk factor present.

- **Varicella:** Ages ≥19, 2 doses (0, 4-8 weeks); Ages ≥50, 2 doses (0, 4-8 weeks) if some risk factor present.

- **Influenza:** Ages ≥19, 1 dose annually if risk factor present; Ages ≥50, 1 dose annually.

- **Pneumoccoccal:** Ages 19-64 if some risk factor present; Ages ≥65, 1 dose.

- **Hepatitis A:** Ages ≥19, 2 doses (0, 6-12 mos., or 0, 6-18 mos.) if some risk factor present.

- **Hepatitis B:** Ages ≥19, 3 doses (0, 1-2 mos., or 0, 4-6 mos.) if some risk factor present.

- **Meningococcal:** Ages ≥19, 1 or more doses if some risk factor present.

Listen to Your Body

The following symptoms should alert you that something is wrong and requires action:

- **Head:** A headache associated with any of the following symptoms can be a sign of high blood pressure, brain hemorrhage, stroke, tumor, meningitis, Lyme disease, or migraine headache (see a doctor immediately):
    - Persists for more than 72 hours
    - Prevents you from doing normal activities
    - Is accompanied by vision or coordination problems
    - Causes difficulty talking or thinking clearly
    - Is associated with arm and leg weakness, fever, or vomiting.

- **Chest:** If chest pain that lasts more than a few minutes, gets worse with exertion or sweating, nausea or shortness of breath, or pain that radiates to the jaw, neck, or arms, it can be signs of a heart attack, angina, or inflammation of the tissue sac surrounding the heart. Seek medical attention immediately. Better to be safe than sorry. If you feel that you may be having a heart attack and there is no telephone or person nearby to offer you first aid or CPR, try coughing on the way to the hospital; it will help to keep your heart pumping!

- **Neck:** If a severe sore throat that gets progressively worse and makes breathing or swallowing difficult, especially if accompanied by swollen glands in the neck or a fever of 101 or higher, it can be signs of infection from mononucleosis or strep throat.

- **Abdomen:** If pain is sudden and severe, last more than 4 days, is only temporarily relieved by eating or recurs with constipation or diarrhea and bloating, it can be signs of appendicitis, gallbladder problems, ulcers, food poisoning, irritable bowel syndrome.

- **Back:** If pain last more than 72 hours or is severe enough to interfere with work or radiates down the leg, any unexplained numbness or tingling accompanied by muscle weakness, it may indicate a herniated disk.

- **Genitals:** If urination is frequent or it is difficult starting or stopping the flow of urine, it may indicate benign prostate enlargement or prostate cancer. A testicle that's tender to touch or feels harder than usual or uneven may indicate infection or testicular cancer, a disease that is 95% curable if discovered early.

- **Skin:** If any sore doesn't heal within a week, or a mole or birthmark bleeds, develops irregular borders or changes color, size or texture, it may indicate skin cancer.

Recommended Regular Physical Exams (by age) for Men

- **Age 20-29:** Blood pressure tests and teeth checked every year. Physical exam of eyes, ears, neck, chest, thyroid, abdomen, chest and lymph nodes, hernia, testicles and penis, reflex and strength tests every 3 years. TB test every 5 years.

- **Age 30-39:** Blood pressure tests and teeth checked every year. Physical exam, blood and urine tests, ECG, and, if you have high cholesterol or a family history of heart disease, cholesterol tests every 3 years.

- **Age 40-49:** Blood pressure tests, digital rectal exam (DRE) to test for prostate cancer, Hemoccult (blood in stool) for colorectal cancer, chest x-ray (if smoker), prostate specific antigen (PSA) tests for prostate cancer (if family history or African American), and teeth checked every year. Physical exam, blood tests, urine test every 2 years. ECG and, if you have high cholesterol or a family history of heart disease, cholesterol tests every 3 years.

- **Age 50+:** Physical exam, blood pressure test, blood tests, urine tests, DRE and PSA tests, and Hemoccult, and teeth checked every year. ECG and sigmoidoscopy for colorectal cancer every 3 years.

Prostate Exam

Men over age 40 should have a yearly digital rectal exam to check the prostate gland for hard or lumpy areas. The doctor feels the prostate through the wall of the rectum.

The keys to prostate health are getting regular exercise, managing stress levels, taking stretch and activity (and breathing) breaks. It also involves eating a low fat, higher-fiber, more vegetarian, and wholesome diet, and avoiding excess use of refined sugars, red meats, and alcohol, while obtaining adequate essential fatty acids daily, such as flaxseed oil. Zinc, vitamins B, C, and E, and particularly B6 are important for a healthy prostate.

Simple 3-Step Testicular Self-Exam

Testicular cancer occurs most often between ages 15 and 34. Most of these cancers are found when men do a testicular self-exam.

- Grasp each testicle between your thumb and first two fingers with your thumb behind the testicle.

- Gently run your fingers around the circumference of each testicle, feeling for any lumps or hard places. The testicles should have the feel of a small hard-boiled egg without its shell.

- At the back of each testicle, where your thumb is, you'll find a lump called the epididymis. It belongs there; the rest of the surface should be smooth and rubbery. If you find a lump of any type anywhere else, see your doctor immediately and ask for a referral to an urologist. Also call your doctor if you feel any soreness or swelling.

Recommended Regular Physical Exams for Women

Age-Related Exams

Here are guidelines for how often you should get a routine checkup. If you have any on-going health problems, you should probably see your health care provider more often.

- **Age 18-39:** A breast exam, Pap test (after you have had three normal Pap smears, ask your health care provider about how often you should have it done), and teeth checked every year. Blood pressure tests, height and weight measurement, and exams to look for cancers of the thyroid, lymph nodes, ovaries, and skin every 2 to 3 years. Cholesterol checks every 5 years. Make sure you are up to date on your shots for rubella (measles) and tetanus (every 10 years).

- **Age 40-65:** An exam to look for cancers of the breast, skin, thyroid, ovaries, lymph nodes, and rectum, a Pap test (ask your health care provider about how often you should have it done), and teeth checked every year. Blood pressure tests, height and weight measurement, stool sample checked for blood, mammogram (after you're 50 years old, you should have a mammogram every year), and an eye exam (with a check for glaucoma) every 1 to 2 years. Cholesterol checks, blood sugar checks, and special tests (sigmoidoscopy or colonoscopy) for colon cancer after age 50 every 3 to 5 years. Remember to get tetanus shot every 10 years.

- **Age 65+:** Have teeth checked every 6 months. Have weight measurement, blood pressure tests, a mammogram, and an exam to look for cancers of the skin, breast, thyroid, ovaries, uterus, lymph nodes, and rectum every year. Check of blood count, cholesterol, blood sugar, hearing and vision (with a check for glaucoma), and Pap tests if you have had abnormal results before every 1 to 3 years. Have tests (sigmoidoscopy or colonoscopy) for colon cancer every 5 years. Get flu shots every year, pneumonia shot if you have not had one before, and tetanus shot every 10 years.

Breast Exam

When breast cancer is found early, a woman has more treatment choices and a good chance of complete recovery. So it is important that breast cancer be detected as early as possible. The National Cancer Institute encourages women to take an active part in early detection. They should talk to their doctor about this disease, the symptoms to watch for, and an appropriate schedule of checkups. Women should ask their doctor about:

- Mammograms (x-rays of the breast)
- Breast exams by a doctor or nurse
- Breast self-examination (BSE)

A mammogram can often show tumors or changes in the breast before they can be felt or cause symptoms. However, mammograms cannot find every abnormal area in the breast. Between visits to the doctor, women should examine their breasts every month. Learning what looks and feels normal will enable you to recognize and find changes. Report any changes to the doctor. Most breast lumps are not cancers, but only a doctor can make a diagnosis.

Pelvic Exam

Regular pelvic exams and Pap tests are important to detect early cancer of the cervix. In a pelvic exam, the doctor feels the uterus, vagina, ovaries, fallopian tubes, bladder, and rectum for any change in size or shape.

For the Pap test, a sample of cells is collected from the upper vagina and cervix with a small brush or a flat wooden stick. The sample is placed on a glass slide and checked under a microscope for cancer or other abnormal cells.

Women should start having a Pap test every year after they turn 18 or become sexually active. If the results are normal for 3 or more years in a row, a woman may have this test less often, based on her doctor's advice.

Ovarian Cancer Blood Test (!Important!): Women should ask their doctor about the CA-125 blood test for ovarian cancer. One out of every 55 women will get ovarian or primary peritoneal cancer, even if they have had their ovaries removed! The "classic" symptoms are an abdomen that suddenly enlarges and constipation and/or diarrhea.

Recommended Vaccines and Physical Exams for Children

Scheduling vaccinations for your children can be confusing. Many vaccines require several doses. Sometimes, due to shortages of vaccines or other issues, a child can get off schedule. The specific vaccines for each age group are based on recommendations from the Centers for Disease Control and Prevention and other leading organizations. If your child misses a dose of a particular vaccine, do not worry. Simply ask your child's doctor about catch-up vaccines.

- **Birth to 4 months:** Hepatitis B – doses 1 and 2 of 3.
  The timing of the first dose of hepatitis B vaccine depends on whether the mother is infected with the hepatitis B virus (HBV) at the time of delivery. If you're HBV-positive, your baby needs the first dose of vaccine along with hepatitis B immune globulin within 12 hours of birth. Even if you're HBV-negative, your baby might receive the first dose of hepatitis B vaccine before leaving the hospital. The second dose of hepatitis B vaccine is given at least one month after the first dose.

- **2 months:** Diphtheria, Tetanus and Acellular Pertussis (DTaP) – dose 1 of 5; Haemophilus Influenzae type b (Hib) – dose 1 of 4; Inactivated Poliovirus (IPV) – dose 1 of 4; Pneumococcal Conjugate (PCV7) – dose 1 of 4; Rotavirus Vaccine – dose 1 of 3.

  At age 2 months, your baby receives the first in a series of several shots designed to offer protection from many diseases. To develop immunity, your baby needs several doses of each vaccine in the months to come. To reduce the number of shots, ask your baby's doctor about combination vaccines. For children who must avoid the pertussis vaccine, combination vaccines are available without it. Timing is especially important for the rotavirus vaccine. The first dose is recommended at age 2 months. The vaccine series **can't** be started after age 3 months.

- **4 months**: Diphtheria, Tetanus and Acellular Pertussis (DTaP) – dose 2 of 5; Haemophilus Influenzae type b (Hib) – dose 2 of 4; Inactivated Poliovirus (IPV) – dose 2 of 4; Pneumococcal Conjugate (PCV7) – dose 2 of 4; Rotavirus Vaccine – Dose 2 of 3.

At the 4-month checkup, your baby receives follow-up doses to those vaccines received at the 2-month checkup. To reduce the number of shots, ask your baby's doctor about combination vaccines.

- **6 months**: Diphtheria, Tetanus and Acellular Pertussis (DTaP) – dose 3 of 5; Haemophilus Influenzae type b (Hib) – dose 3 of 4; Pneumococcal Conjugate (PCV7) – dose 3 of 4; Rotavirus Vaccine – dose 3 of 3.

At the 6-month checkup, your baby receives another round of the vaccines given at 2 months and 4 months, with the exception of the polio vaccine. The third dose of polio vaccine comes a little later in the vaccines schedule. Again, ask your baby's doctor about combination vaccines to reduce the number of shots.

- **6 months-18 months**: Hepatitis B – dose 3 of 3; Inactivated Poliovirus (IPV) – dose 3 of 4.

Unless your baby's hepatitis B vaccine series began in the newborn nursery, he or she receives the final dose of vaccine at this time. For full effectiveness, the final dose of hepatitis B vaccine is given at least eight weeks after your baby receives the second dose. The last dose of hepatitis B vaccine **shouldn't** be given to children younger than age 6 months. Your baby's doctor may recommend giving the polio vaccine at around age 9 months to avoid giving four shots at the 6-month checkup.

- **6 months-59 months**: Influenza – annual dose.

An annual influenza vaccine protects your child from the flu. This yearly vaccine is especially important for children between ages 6 months and 59 months because they're among those most likely to be hospitalized for complications of the flu. In the first year that your child receives a flu shot, two doses are required, spaced one month apart. In the following years, only one dose of vaccine is needed. The vaccine is available each fall and provides protection during the upcoming flu season.

- **12 months-15 months**: Haemophilus Influenzae type b (Hib) – dose 4 of 4; Pneumoncoccal Conjugate (PCV7) – dose 4 of 4; Measles-Mumps-Rubella (MMR) – dose 1 of 2; Chickenpox (varicella) – dose 1 of 2.

The final doses of both Hib and PCV7 vaccines must wait until your child is age 12 months or older. The first doses of MMR and varicella vaccines also are given at this time. To avoid giving four shots in one visit, your child's doctor may recommend the MMR and varicella vaccines at age 12 months and the Hib and PCV7 vaccines at age 15 months. It's also common to combine the MMR and varicella vaccines in a single shot.

- **12 months-23 months**: Hepatitis A – 2 doses

The hepatitis A vaccine is recommended for all children at age 12 months, with the two doses in the series given at least six months apart.

- **15 months-18 months**: Diphtheria, Tetanus and Acellular Pertussis (DTaP) – dose 4 of 5.

Your child should receive the fourth dose of DTaP between ages 15 months and 18 months. In some cases, the fourth dose can be given as early as age 12 months, as long as it's been six months since the last dose.

• **4 years-6 years**: Diphtheria, Tetanus and Acellular Pertussis (DTaP) – dose 5 of 5; Inactivated Poliovirus (IPV) – dose 4 of 4; Measles-Mumps-Rubella (MMR) – dose 2 of 2; Chickenpox (varicella) – dose 2 of 2.

About the time your child starts kindergarten, he or she should receive the final doses of DTaP, IPV, MMR and varicella vaccines. Many states require proof of current vaccinations before allowing school enrollment. The more children who've been immunized the better the protection of all children in the school from vaccine-preventable diseases.

• **11 years-12 years**: Human Papillomavirus (HPV), for girls – 3 doses; Meningococcal Conjugate Vaccine (MCV4) – 1 dose; Tetanus Toxoid, reduced Diphtheria Toxoid and Acellular Pertussis (Tdap) – 1 dose.

The human Papillomavirus vaccine offers protection from the viruses that cause genital warts and most cervical cancers. The vaccine is intended for girls ages 11 to 12, but it may be used in girls as young as age 9. The vaccine is given as a series of three injections over a six-month period. The second dose is given two months after the first dose, followed four months later by the third dose. A catch-up immunization is recommended for girls ages 13 to 26 who haven't been vaccinated or who haven't completed the full vaccine series. MCV4 is recommended for children age 11 and older and for unvaccinated adolescents when they enter high school, about age 15. College freshmen living in dormitories who haven't previously received the meningococcal vaccine also should be vaccinated with MCV4 or with meningococcal polysaccharide vaccine (MPSV4). If your child has completed the childhood DTP/DTaP vaccination series but hasn't received a Td booster shot, he or she should have the booster shot at age 11 to 12. Follow-up doses are recommended every 10 years.

Chapter 10

Successful Parole Tips, Rules, and Actions

"It is a prerogative and a privilege of man to become guilty and realize his guilt, but also his responsibility to overcome guilt by rising above it, by growing beyond yourselves, by changing for the better."
– Viktor Frankl, *Man's Search for Meaning*

NOT ALL STATES have a parole system and guidelines vary from state to state. When you are paroled, you serve part of your prison sentence under the supervision of your community.

To you, and all those around you, life on parole can be inconvenient, restrictive, annoying, invasive, undignified, and unforgiving for those who break the rules. On the other hand, so is life in prison. Parole can be a better alternative to prison for those who obey all rules and laws...even when nobody is looking. An overwhelming majority of parole violations happen when parolees obey only 75-99 percent of the rules and laws.

The successful person obeys all rules and laws, refuses to be diverted off course, and turns the negatives of parole into a positive source of motivation and inspiration.

Parole is a "conditional" liberty, with many parole conditions. It is an extension of incarceration. Nevertheless, it is an opportunity to be with family and friends; to be responsible, work, and pay taxes.

Parole can be tougher and more complicated than doing time in prison. Inside you time is managed; outside you must manage your time. Inside it matters little whether you work or obtain training and education; outside, you must. Parole demands that you stay focused because distractions, temptations, and toxic peers can lead to re-incarceration...and possible STRIKES!

This chapter offers only a glimpse of available programs for parolees. For more specific information about state or Federal programs, contact the parole department in your area.)

Tips and Rules for Making Parole
- **Keep good oral, written, and phone records – when, whom, and what:** Keep a pocket calendar to record your activities. Keep in touch with your parole agent, especially reporting positive changes in your life. Use registered mail when writing to your parole agent. Keep good tool and household inventory.

- **Follow written parole rules:** Never allow a "familiar" relationship to exist between you and your work supervisor or parole agent. Immediately notify your parole agent of any change of address, even if it's next door, and job(s) such as changes in working hours, location, a second job or multiple jobs, or work with other parolees.

- **Don't look for trouble:** Returning to old familiar places – bar, liquor store, neighborhood hangouts, or with old crime partners – or not showing up for work, or not informing parole agent of your activities can result in a violation.

- **Don't play the drug game, or be a risk taker:** It's always the first drink of alcohol, the first joint, snort, or even the first negative thought that results in relapse and recidivism.

- **Don't fall for the new materialism:** When your behavior is driven by the desire for pleasure, power, or prosperity, you have taken the first step to eliminating masking meaning and purpose in your life. Ultimately, these may lead to depression, aggression, and addiction.

- **Don't fall back into old habits that lead back to jail or prison:** Falling back into old habits is like throwing rocks at the prison walls and yelling, "Let me back in!" Don't drive through old familiar neighborhoods in order to get a "scent." When you do, you've already relapsed mentally and physically. You cannot return to your old surroundings **until** you have learned to survive in a new environment, support system, and thinking process. It matters not where you parole to; it matters only what you do there.

- **Life is not a beer commercial:** To sell, you must create a need. Beer, cigarettes, drug and auto commercials sell **instant** pleasure, power, and prosperity. Don't fall victim to the false promises.

- **Have goals that lead to rewards, not rewards that lead to scams:** Focus on your family and being present 24/7, 365 days a year. Give back to your community; teach somebody to read; volunteer to paint a senior citizen's home; speak to children in schools and churches about making poor choices.

- **Focus on the process, not the obstacles:** Life is a process of living one moment, one day at a time. The past and future are beyond your control. Do not make promises to remain clean and sober for life, only for today.

- **Focus on restoring meaning and purpose to your life:** The leading cause of depression, aggression towards others and self, and addiction is the lack of meaning in one's life. Know that all experiences, encounters with others and loves, creative works and deeds, and fate are unavoidable gifts and benefit you unless you choose to not learn the unique lessons intended for you. You may not recognize the lesson immediately. Just accept the fact and, sooner and much later, you will come to know the truth. Otherwise, the symbolic lesson will be played out repeatedly.

Achieve a Successful Parole

- "Freedom" is not freedom from, but freedom to take on the responsibilities of community life and must be realized **slowly**. Remember: Long-lasting change moves like a glacier; if change occurs too quickly, watch your back!

- The **will to pleasure, power, and prosperity** must be replaced with the **will to meaning**. This is obtained one day at a time through an open attitude of gratefulness, a job, community volunteer work, and being **present** in your family's life 24/7. Neither presents nor gifts can ever replace your presence in their lives. The lure of criminal activity lies in its promise to provide power, domination, manipulation, diversion of pain, and wanton pleasure. In the words of David Lewis, President of "Free At Last" in East Palo Alto: "(Criminal activity) causes me to break out in spots, spots like Folsom, San Quentin, and Pelican Bay State Prisons."

- There is only one **power**, the power to save someone. And there is only one **honor**, the honor to help someone. And there are only two **races**, the race of good, decent men and women, and the race of bad ones.

- Seek out or start up a parolee support group that meets regularly to address the issues of readjustment.

- Seek out or start up a parolee car pool for getting to and from work.

- Enroll in academic, vocational, and classes that match your hobbies or other interests.

- Participate on a regular basis in programs that enrich your spiritual side.

General Conditions of Parole

- Should you violate conditions of your parole, you are subject to arrest, suspension, and/or revocation of your parole.

- You waive extradition from any part of the U.S. and will not contest any effort to return you to your state of parole jurisdiction.

- You may be placed in a community treatment facility or state prison if you pose a danger to yourself or others.

- A parole agent or any law enforcement officer may search you and your residence and any property under your control without a warrant.

- You may be released to the custody of another jurisdiction that has lodged a detainer against you. You are to immediately contact the nearest parole office should you be released prior to the expiration of your parole.

- You may request that your parole agent or an attorney assist you in obtaining a certificate of rehabilitation, which may lead to a partial or full pardon.

- Any change of residence shall be reported to your parole agent in advance.

- You shall comply with all instructions of your parole agent and will not travel more than the specified distance from your residence without his/her approval.

You will not be absent from your county of residence longer than the specified period of time. You will not leave the state of jurisdiction without prior written approval of your parole agent.

- You shall not engage in conduct prohibited by law.

- You shall not own, use, have access to, or have under your control any type of firearm or instrument or device that a reasonable person would believe to be capable of being used as a firearm. You shall not own, use, have access to, or have under your control any ammunition that could be used in a firearm. You shall not own, use, have access to, or have under your control any knife with a blade longer than two inches. An exception to this are kitchen knives that must be kept in your residence and knives related to your employment that may be used and carried only in connection with your employment, or crossbow of any kind.

Pre-Parole Things to Do

- Apply for a parole transfer if warranted, six month beforehand. "Warranted" means that you meet the immediate family criteria. It means that you have a verified job offer whereas a comparable one is not available in your county of commitment. Or, it can mean that you have been accepted into an academic, vocational, or rehabilitation program, whereas a comparable one is not available in your county of commitment.

- Apply for credit restoration as soon as you are eligible.

- Ask your counselor to help you in having active warrants and traffic tickets dismissed.

- If you are eligible, take the test for your General Education Development certificate (GED). If not, make a big effort to study for the exam. While on parole, you can enroll in adult education classes, literacy classes in a library or employment office.

- Apply for your Social Security card. It takes about two weeks to process and will be forwarded to you at a parole address (can be the parole office).

- Fill out an application for employment assistance.

- Fill out a Pell grant application to cover the costs of tuition, books, and tools while attending a college or a trade school.

- Keep in contact with family, friends, and former employers, and maintain a positive attitude.

- Write to your parole agent, or "To Whom It Concerns," at least 60 days before you parole. Give any updated information and discuss your parole plans.

- Plan to make the best of the initial Parole Orientation meeting. In some instances, this is in addition to your initial office visit and testing.

- Most important, keep a good attitude and stay active in prisons programs up to the last day.

Post-Release Things to Do

- Report directly to your parole office. If you are unable to report, you must immediately notify your parole office.

- You must obey all laws when traveling form prison to your home. If you are arrested, tell the officer you are on parole. Notify your parole office of the arrest; it does not like surprise notices from other agencies.

- Do not waste the release money given to you when you leave from prison. Use the money wisely for basic needs, such as food, shelter, and travel. Check in with the parole office immediately upon your arrival if you are in need of emergency shelter.

- If you are stranded out of town and unable to return to your community, contact the nearest parole office. Explain the problem to them. Also, you must contact your parole office to report the situation. Remember it is your responsibility to get transportation to your community.

- If someone commits a crime against you, notify the police and your parole agent of the crime.

- Freedom must be slowly regained. Do not celebrate that which is not quite yours. For example, do not celebrate your release from prison with drugs, alcohol, or other questionable activities. Remember that freedom is not regained by being 99.9 % honest with yourself and others. Many are violated for being only 0.1 % dishonest.

Registering With the Police and Sheriff

- If you have been convicted of a sex, drug, or arson crime, you are required by law to register at your local police or sheriff's station. You must give your home address to the police and sign a registration form. If you have questions, speak to your parole agent. Failure to register within five days for sex offenses will result in a 'strike'!

- In some states, you must maintain registration for sex offenses for life unless you receive a pardon.

- In some states, you must maintain registration for drug offenses for five years beyond your parole discharge date.

Removing Tattoos

Tattoo-removal resources may be found at the following websites.

- www.tattooremoval.org
- www.tattooremoval.com
- www.cleanslatela.org
- www.beyondthestreets.org
- www.tat2begone.com
- www.tattooremovalinstitute.org

Chapter 11

Lifelong Finance and Budgeting

A debt never gets too old for an
honest person to pay.

THIS CHAPTER DISCUSSES personal lifelong finance and budgeting. Personal finance and budget planning involves planning a budget, paying off debts, saving for a major life event and saving for retirement. Planning your finances is essential to having success in parole as well as in other areas such as relationships, health and your professional life. Being in control of your finances gives you a feeling of satisfaction and provides you with confidence because you will ultimately have more choices in your personal and professional life, while resisting temptations.

It is never too late to start finance planning for the future. Whether you are in your 20s, 30, 40s, or older, setting goals and planning is important. For instance, in your twenties, you may be planning a budget from a new job and saving an emergency fund. In your 30s, you may be saving for a home. In your 40s, you may be budgeting and saving for long-term retirement. In your 50s and 60s, perhaps your goals are to save for a lifelong wish such as a world vacation. At any age, planning and budgeting your finances in addition to being aware of how to achieve goals will be very beneficial.

You'll find a wealth of information about general financial planning at your local library and on the Internet. Many books and websites offer general information on financial planning, savings and investments, taxes, financing your retirement, paying for college and other topics. Others also provide financial calculators that can guide you through the process of calculating financial resources you will need in the future, such as how to pay for a child's college education or finance your retirement. There are also several commercial software programs that offer this type of interactive calculator.

One caution when researching information on the Internet: Make sure the source is a reliable and known entity, as anyone can set up a website and claim to be a financial expert.

A few good places to start your Internet search are the following sites:
- The American Savings Education Council   www.asec.org/ballpark.htm
- Deloitte and Touche, LLP   www.dtonline.com/prptoc/prptoc.htm
- The Money Advisor   www.moneyadvisor.com
- Investor Home   www.investorhome.com
- MONEY Magazine   www.money.com

Also, use web search engines such as Yahoo!, Google, and Bing and ente
such as "financial planning" or "retirement planning."

Steps to Take for Debt-Free Holidays

- Plan ahead. Buy a few gifts each month all during the year, or set aside a
  money each payday for a major shopping blowout with cash in hand. Leav
  credit cards at home.
- If you do charge items, pay off the charge in one payment.
- Plan a detailed holiday budget for the months of October (Halloween), Novem
  (Thanksgiving), December (Christmas), and January (after-Christmas sales).
- Make a gift list, including how much you can spend on each person. Do not devia
  from the amount set.
- Send cards instead of gifts. Better yet, make your own cards.
- Make goodies or craft items and give those as gifts.
- Give practical items rather than items for entertainment.
- Don't get pressured into making a purchase you can't afford just because it's a
  good deal or on sale.

How to Get a Handle on Your Debt

- Don't carry a checkbook, credit cards, or ATM cards. Use cash.
- Never use credit cards for cash advances. It just increases your debt and the
  interest rates are often higher.
- Plan a reasonable budget that includes extras (periodic entertainment/gifts/
  insurance payments/other expenses).
- Couples should plan budgets together so that they both know where the
  money goes.
- Set up an emergency fund, even if it's just $10 a week.
- Stick to your food-shopping list or get a responsible family member or friend to
  do your shopping. Write out the shopping list before leaving the house and never
  shop for food when you are hungry!
- Wait 24 hours before ordering something from a catalog order call. If you can't
  remember what it was you wanted, you can surely live without it!

Clothing

Buy clothes, shoes, coats, kitchen supplies and furniture at second hand/thrift stores at
substantial savings. Check out those stores that are on the affluent side of the community.

Food

- **Cooking:** Cook and bake from scratch.
- **Coupons:** Clip and save, but also compare brands and prices. Check <u>www.</u>

thegrocerygame.com for other coupon sources. In one case, a $154 shopping bill whittled down by $148 in coupons allowed the shopper to spend only $6 for her groceries! Every week the website tips you off to the best sales at your local grocery store and how to maximize those sales with coupons you get from the paper. Subscribing to the grocery game website costs $5.00 a month. A less expensive website is www.thegrocerygame.com, but it does not maximize your coupons the way grocerygame does. The grocerygame site works but not for everybody.

- **Buying:** Buy generic brands. Buy in bulk.

- **General Food Shopping List and Tips:** The following list is for people who have to buy their food on a week-to-week basis. If you can shop once or twice a month, you will have more money to buy items that are on sale and stock up at that time. You will have to watch for specials in your area and to make full use of things such as double-coupons or places such as food warehouses and outlets. Pick up all of the flyers from stores in your area when you are out for other reasons such as on your way to or from work. Check store windows and signs for specials. Make out your shopping list and menu for the week, taking into consideration all of the items that are on sale. You may have to change your shopping habits, but the amount of savings will be worth it in the long run.

  - **Every-Week Stuff:** Spend between $40 and $50 on milk, eggs, margarine, bread, meat, juice, sauces, vegetables, fruit, and pasta.
  - **Longer-Lasting Stuff:** Spend between $30 and $40 on powdered milk, flour, potatoes, rice, cornmeal, oatmeal, cream of wheat, spices, peanut butter, jellies, jams, cooking oil, laundry soap, salt, and syrups.
  - **Stock-Up Stuff:** Spend between $20 and $30 on good buys. Buy **generic** rather than **brand** name at **outlet stores** rather than **chain stores**.

Entertainment

Take advantage of public services, matinee movie rates, videos, picnics, walks, parks, and recreation.

Garage/Estate Sales

When you have accumulated things that have served their purpose and are no longer in general use, dispose of them in this manner to generate extra cash and clean up your environment.

Best Months to Buy Certain Items

The wheels of commerce turn with predictable regularity on an annual basis. The key is to time your purchase.

- **January:** Christmas and New Year bargains; men's suits, linens; appliances and furniture.
- **February:** Big reductions on china, glass, silver, mattresses, and bedding.
- **March:** Preseason promotions for spring clothing; ski equipment at an annual low.

- **April:** Sales begin after Easter on clothing.
- **May:** Specials on household cleaning products; carpets and rugs.
- **June:** Semiannual sale on furniture.
- **July:** Liquidation of sportswear and sporting equipment. Sale on garden tools and supplies.
- **August:** Clearance on current car models. Also, equipment linked to summer season is marked down (patio furniture, lawn mowers, and yard tools, BBQ and camping equipment).
- **September:** Best deals on school clothes at the end of the month.
- **October:** Best month to do your Christmas shopping.
- **November:** Wool clothes (women's coats/men's suits).
- **December:** Next to August, this is the best month to buy a car.

Three Ways to Avoid Overspending

- Don't charge to the limit on each card and then go on to your next credit card.
- Don't use cards for small purchases – pay cash.
- Don't focus on paying a monthly minimum and thus incur high finance charges and potential long-term indebtedness.

Food (15-20%)
Laundromat _____
Other _____
Total WAM _____ (Multiply this by 4.3 to obtain monthly WAM)
Monthly Expense Budget Worksheet (Average this over 3-6 months)

Budget Item	Budgeted	Expense
WAM	_____	_____
Housing (20-30%)	_____	_____
(Mortgage/Rent/Taxes/		
Repairs/Improvements)		
Child Care	_____	_____
Support Payments	_____	_____
Telephone (Basic)	_____	_____
Utilities (4-7%)	_____	_____
Auto (6-20%)	_____	_____
(Gas/Oil/Repair/Ins./		

(continues next page)

Parking/Public Transportation)

Medical (2-8%)   _____   _____

Invest. and Savings (5-10%)   _____   _____

Clothing (4%)   _____   _____

Monthly Installment(15-20%)   _____   _____

Total Cost of Survival   _____   _____

Take-home Pay – Total Cost of Survival = Savings   _____

Building a Budget

Weekly "Walk around Money" (WAM) Expense Worksheet

The items below are paid in cash. The "WAM" is the key to successfully controlling a budget. So pay close attention to developing these figures.

Buying a Car

A Four-Step Process

- **First,** have a make, model, and price limit in mind.

- **Second,** find out the basic dealer cost. Refer to the NADA Yellow Book, the Kelley Blue Book, or a Consumer Reports Buying Guide.

- **Third,** rent the specific car in which you re interested for a week to get a true feel of the vehicle. Most buyers will skip this step.

- **Fourth,** strive for a 15-20 percent reduction in the asking price through negotiation. Dealerships usually mark up the price of the car by this margin. Expect to pay about 4 percent above actual dealer cost.

Other Helpful Hints

- The vehicle identification number, or VIN, gives the year, body style, transmission and engine cylinders of a car. One is inside the door jamb on the driver's side and the other is mounted on the dash near the windshield, also on the driver's side. If it has been altered or removed, buyer beware. You can also use the VIN to check the car's history, for example, if it has ever been in a wreck.

- Shop for a new car near the end of the month. Salespeople, eager to meet their sales quota, are most likely to negotiate with you. Early fall inventory sales are also advantageous. Refrain from showing excitement over a particular model and be wary of falling victim to salespeople and manager manipulation. There will be those who will be direct with you and others who will not.

- The finance manager's job is twofold:
1. To help you finish paperwork and/or arrange for financing.
2. To sell you add-on products such as
   - Extended warranties that are largely unnecessary.
   - Credit life insurance that may be overpriced by as much as 800%! Shop around and save.
   - Rust-proofing, which the car usually comes with from the factory.
   - Auto seat fabric protection that may cost as much as $200-300. Buy Scotch Guard for a few dollars and save a great deal.

- Ask for a simple interest loan. Avoid compounding interest and Rule-of-78 loans. Finance a car for no more than 3-4 years. Keep the car long enough to pay off the loan. Then continue to make car payments to yourself for full-cash purchase of your next car.

- Avoid taking out a second mortgage on your home to purchase a car. You run the risk of losing your home through loan default if you begin to miss payments.

- A good used, one-owner car is desirable transportation while you save and locate the car you really want.

- Plan to buy a car that you will enjoy 5 to 7 years or longer, rather than buying frequently and losing money through depreciation.

- Buy good used cars through estate, city, county, state, and federal auctions. Also, consider storage unit and customs auctions. Lastly, check the classified ads in the newspaper for listings of local auctions.

- The 2011 estimate by AAA puts the annual average cost of owning and operating a car at $9,000, based on the costs of gas, oil, tires, maintenance, insurance, registration, taxes and financing. This composite average is based on three cars driven 15,000 miles a year. Compare that cost with the convenience of public transportation. For example, a bus ticket would cost less than 10 percent of that annually.

Insuring a Car

Auto insurance costs may be divided into three major groups. They are listed here from least expensive to most expensive:

1. **Direct-to-Consumer Companies:** Lowest operation cost and no commission.
   - 21st Century 1-800-211-7283 i21.com
   - GEICO 1-800-861-8380 geico.com
   - USAA 1-800-531-8080 usaa.com

2. **Captive-Agents Companies:** Represent the company, not you.
   - AllState 1-877-597-0570 allstate.com
   - AAA aaa.com
   - Farmers 1-323-932-3200 farmers.com
   - State Farm 1-661-663-1000 statefarm.com

3. **Independent-Agents or Brokers:** Place business with several companies. May charge additional fee.
   - Mercury 1-800-579-3467 mercuryinsurance.com
   - Progressive 1-800-260-3534 progressive.com
   - Safeco 1-206-545-5000 safeco.com

4. **Bad Driving Record (?):** No matter how bad your driving record, you can get insurance through the California Automobile "Assigned Risk Plan" at 1-800-622-0954 or www.aipso.com/ca.

5. **Low Income and Living in S.F./L.A.:** If you live in the city or county of San Francisco or Los Angeles, an area of Good Driver and have a low income, you may be eligible for the "Low-Cost- Auto Insurance" program. Contact CAARP at 1-800-622-0954 or aipso.com/ca.

Steps to Buying a Home

When you consider that your house payment could be as low as your current rent, then you simply must take advantage of the opportunities available to you, particularly if you are a first-time home buyer. Additionally, there are tax advantages to owning a home.

- **Step 1 – Loan Pre-Qualification:** Home loan officers can do a quick loan pre-qualification in person or over the phone. This identifies any problems you may have to overcome during the loan and escrow process as well as set a price range that you can work with during the home search.

- **Step 2 – Loan Application:** You should then meet with your lender, fill out a complete loan application and have your credit report run. This is the smartest way to go. By getting your entire loan information going first, you can have a near loan approval before you even look at a home. This is almost like shopping with *cash*. And it also gives you a lot of bargaining power with the seller!

- **Step 3 – Home Search:** When you get the word back from the lender that your loan application looks good (or good enough at this point), a computerized computer search of the Multiple Listing Service for all the homes that fit your need and budget is conducted. It is better for you to preview the homes from the exterior and check out the neighborhoods on your own, without a realtor pressuring you to buy *now*. A computerized printout and map of each property can be provided to you. When you have narrowed the search down to your favorite homes, each can then be opened up for you to see the inside. The goal is to find you a home where you're going to be happy.

- **Step 4 – The Offer:** Once you've found a home you wish to buy, you and your realtor will structure an offer with an aim at: 1) getting you the very best deal possible and 2) getting the offer accepted.

- **Step 5 – The Escrow Period:** Once the offer is accepted, escrow will be opened with a title company. It's during this period that the appraisal on the home is ordered, the required pest control inspection is done, the title to your home is researched, and your loan package, with all its verifications, is completed.

- **Step 6 – Underwriting:** When everything in Step 5 is complete, the loan package goes to an underwriter to verify that all items have been completed. Since most loans are sold to the government, your loan must meet certain guidelines before the government will buy it. It's the underwriter's job and responsibility to make sure your loan, and the home itself, meets those guidelines. So, expect many, seemingly silly and useless forms and requirements prior to loan acceptance!

- **Step 7 – The Signing:** When the package comes back from the underwriter, both you and the seller (at separate times) are scheduled to come into the title company to sign all the documents and to bring in any funds which may be due to close escrow.

- **Step 8 – The Lender Review:** The signed documents now go back to the lender to make sure everything has been properly endorsed and to double-check that nothing is missed from the package. If everything is in order, you go to Step 9.

- **Step 9 – Funding and Recording:** The lender now funds the loan and the escrow company takes your deed to the county recorder's office and records your ownership of the home. **You may now move into your home!**

FICO - Financial Risks Credit Re-Scoring for Home Buyers

FICO credit scores are those once-secret, triple-digit numbers that often pigeonhole home-loan applicants as good financial risks or bad. But there is a fast-growing trend that can dramatically improve your loan prospects almost overnight. It is called "rapid re-scoring." This is a service now offered by dozens of local credit reporting agencies around the country that allows mortgage loan officers to request a re-scoring of applicants' credit files at each of the three giant credit repositories - Equifax, Experian, and TransUnion.

At the request of the loan officer, a local credit reporting agency analyzes an applicant's files, obtains written corrections from creditors of any mistaken information in the files, and advises the applicant on how to restructure certain open credit lines in order to raise credit scores. Sometimes scores can be boosted by 40 to 100 points or more in less than a week, all fully within the law, and with the cooperation of the credit repositories themselves.

With a higher score in hand, borrowers then often qualify for lower mortgage rates, lower loan fees, and better terms overall. Corrective re-scoring literally can save consumers tens of thousands of dollars in long-term debts, and alert them to negative information sitting in their credit files.

FICO stands for Fair, Isaac and Co., the developer of the scoring model that ranks applicants in terms of their relative likelihood to pay their debts on time. FICO scores are now easy to obtain. Fair, Isaac and Equifax provide them on the Internet for a nominal charge (www.myfico.com) , and the other repositories provide proprietary scoring advisory information as well.

To qualify for the best loan quotes, borrowers generally need scores of 700 or better. Scores under 620 are "sub-prime" and produce significantly higher quotes on interest rates and fees.

High credit balances relative to card limits are a major no-no for FICO scores. When your limit is $10,000 and you've got a $9,800 balance, your score takes a hit. By paying off or redistributing balances so that no car or credit line has a high balance against the limit, your FICO scores can jump from "a high-risk mortgage applicant" to "an A-plus mortgage applicant."

Habitat for Humanity International: Decent Home at Low Cost

Habitat's goal is to build decent, adequate, and affordable homes in partnership with people in need. Through volunteer labor, management expertise, and tax-deductible donations of money and materials, Habitat builds and rehabilitates homes with the help of potential homeowners. Houses are sold at no profit to partner families, and no-interest (0%) mortgages are issued over a fixed period. Costs of homes differ relative to location, labor, land, and materials, are currently average between $35,000-40,000. Small monthly mortgage payments, including taxes and insurance, are repaid over 7 to 20 years and deposited into a revolving "Fund for Humanity" which supports the construction of more houses.

Habitat is not a giveaway program. Each potential homeowner family is required to invest 500 hours of "sweat equity" (volunteer) hours actually working alongside Habitat volunteers to build their home, or another family's home. This reduces the cost of the house, increases the pride of ownership among family members, and fosters the development of positive relationships with other persons.

Families apply to local Habitat projects. A family selection committee chooses homeowners based on their level of need, their willingness to become partners in the program, and their ability to repay the loan. Every project follows a non-discriminatory policy of family selection. Neither race nor religion is a factor in choosing the families to receive Habitat houses.

For nearest Habitat program, look in the telephone book for Habitat for Humanity, County of _____, depending on the county in which you reside. You may also contact: Habitat for Humanity International, 121 Habitat Street, Americus, Georgia 31709-3498. Habitat Help line: 912-924-6935, x550, 800-334-3308, FAX 912-924-6541. Habitat's catalog, "Sharing Habitat," lists books, brochures, slide shows, video and audio cassettes. You may also request to be placed on the mailing list for *Habitat World*, the official Habitat newspaper that is published bimonthly.

Selling a Home

Selling a home requires professional help or knowledge in order to avoid any legal consequences. Shop around for the best service you can obtain from a real estate brokerage that will also provide you with the greatest profit. An Internal Revenue Service rule allows a married seller of any age to keep up to $500,000 of his or her home-sale profit tax-free. The home must have been held for five years and must have been the seller's primary residence for a total of at least two of the past five years. Single tax-filers can keep up to $250,000 assuming that they meet the same residency requirement.

How to Find a Credit Union

- Find out what credit union, if any, with which your employer has an affiliation.
- Ask your relatives what credit unions they belong to. Many credit unions accept relatives of members.
- Ask if your church, college, or association is affiliated with a credit union.
- If you're interested in a particular credit union, ask about its field of membership and whether you might be eligible to join.

Typical Money-Management Mistakes

New homebuyers often take out a 30-year or 40-year mortgage. Most of their payments in the first 20 to 25 years are applied toward the interest, thus very slowly reducing the mortgage principal. If you must start with a 30-year mortgage, consider refinancing your loan after you have occupied your home for two years. Often the interest rates are much lower on a 10- and 15-year mortgage, while the payments increase only a fraction, thus saving you a tremendous amount in interest. The goal should be to pay off the loan, any loan, as quickly as possible.

Credit card offers come in the mail every day, advertising 18-24% bankcards. Credit cards with interest rates varying between 5 and 12% will often save you 45% or more. Good credit, no credit, or bad credit, check out www.creditcard.com or call 800-344-7714. Keep in mind that 60% of credit-card holders who run monthly balances pay on average 14.7% more for everything they buy. The first step for getting out of debt is to stop borrowing money! Don't add new debt. Cut up the cards.

Instead of whole life insurance, purchase renewable term insurance and save as much as 80%.

Department Store Complaints

Since most department stores are in good standing with the Better Business Bureau, filing a complaint with it may do very little in resolving your problem. If still unresolved, file your complaint instead with the Attorney General's Office.

Applying for Credit: The "Big 8" of a Positive Credit Profile

When seeking a loan of any kind, the lender looks at the following elements of a positive credit profile in order of importance:

- a positive up-to-date credit report
- a home with a mortgage
- an American Express or Diners' Club card
- a job you have held for a year or more
- a current or paid-off bank loan
- a MasterCard or Visa card
- a department store credit card
- a telephone in your own name

Debt Collection Information

- **Negotiating with Your Creditors:** If you have missed one or two payments, contact the creditor before they contact *you*. This shows a good-faith effort to fulfill your obligation. If you explain why you cannot pay your debt now, the creditor may be more willing to renegotiate payment. Make sure you keep copies of any written communication you have, and write down the date and content of all phone calls.

- **Prioritize Your Debts:** List your debts in order of importance. Debt collection can be a scary process. Sometimes people pay a creditor just so they will quit bothering them. However, if you are just getting by and only have enough money to feed and clothe your family, you should not be giving your money to a creditor. Get control of your budget, determine what you need for food, clothing, and health care for you and your family, then work with what you have left over.

- **Debt Collection Agencies:** Your original creditor may turn your debt over to a collection agency. A collection agency is a company that collects past due bills. A creditor is not required to notify you before turning your account over to an agency. If the debt has been assigned to a collection agency, you should assume negotiations with the agency, instead of the original creditor. The collection agency now has the right to collect the debt, even if you pay the original creditor, and can sue you for failure to pay.

- **Your Rights in Avoiding Creditor Harassment and Stopping It Once It Has Started:** If your creditor is contacting you, keep in mind your rights as a consumer. Your creditor will be more and more persistent the longer your debt is past due. You will receive a letter first, then phone calls. There are laws that regulate the behavior of debt collectors.

Fair Debt Collection Practices Act

- **Creditors cannot practice general harassment or intimidation or employ false or misleading information or contact friends, relatives, neighbors, or co-workers about your debt.** They may contact your parents, spouse, or financial adviser about payment of a debt only if a court authorizes it. No debt collector may use obscene or profane language in addressing you. They may not threaten you with force, arrest, or other scare tactics. They may not lie about who they are, call you collect, call before 8:00 a.m. in the morning or after 9:00 p.m. at night, or repeatedly ring and hang up. Your employer and other family members may be contacted only for limited reasons and not for purposes of harassment. Your creditor cannot talk to anyone but you about your debts.

- **Creditors must leave you alone once you've informed them.** You have the right to be left alone. If you do not want to receive phone calls regarding your debts, you can request that a debt collector only contact you by mail. Or you can request that they stop contacting you completely, although it is usually better to maintain some kind of contact and work something out. If you notify the debt collector in writing that you refuse to pay the debt and that you want them to stop contacting you, they must stop. However, this will almost certainly result in your getting sued.

- **You have the right to the truth.** No debt collector may lie to you to convince you to pay a debt. This means, for example, that they cannot tell you a lawsuit is about to be filed against you unless that is true.

- **You have the right to accurate information.** You may demand that you be given a complete run-down of what you owe, to whom, and for what. This must be provided to you in writing. The debt collector without a request on your part should mail it to you, but you certainly have the right to ask for it.

- **You do not have to reveal where you work or where you bank.** If you are asked this information, you do not have to answer. They may not contact you at your place of employment if you object.

Credit Card Bill of Rights

You have the right to:

- Obtain from a credit bureau a report of everything in your credit file.
- Know who has made an inquiry into your credit file.
- Request a credit bureau check and correct any incorrect information in your credit file.
- Get missing credit information added to your file.
- Have detrimental credit information removed from your file after 7 years and bankruptcy information after 10 years. Also check "Length of Time Negative Credit Information Stays on Your Credit Report."
- Put your side of the story on disputed information into your credit file.
- Keep private all information in your file from anyone other than legitimate members of the credit reporting agencies.
- Have your credit report transferred from one area to another any time you move.
- Use small claims courts to resolve any dispute with the credit bureau about incorrect or inaccurate information in your file.
- Know exactly why you were refused credit. You must contact within 10 days the institution refusing the credit. Limit your inquiry to 100 or fewer words.
- Remain silent about poor credit information that does not currently appear in your file.
- If you feel your rights are being violated or that you are a victim of unlawful harassment, you should speak to a lawyer or file a complaint with the Federal Trade Commission.

How to Stop Creditor Harassment

If you feel you are the victim of creditor harassment, you should first send a "cease and desist" letter to the creditor. The following is a sample of a "cease and desist" letter.

As you can see, there are spaces for you to fill in the abuse tactics of the collector or creditors' employees. Describe the emotional distress the abusive tactics are causing. Make sure you keep a copy of the letter you send for your files.

Once the collection agency receives your letter, they are not legally allowed to contact you further, unless they are writing or called to say that all contact will end or to tell you about any specific action they are taking (such as filing a lawsuit). You may want to send a complaint letter to the collector, the state attorney general's office, and a consumer protection agency. These letters generally produce good results because they get the attention of the collection agency or creditor.

Date: Today's Date
To: Name and Address of Creditor or Collection Agency
From: Your Name
RE: Your Account Number

Dear Creditor/Agency:

I am writing to you in order to request that you stop all communications with me about my account with (insert creditor's name). I am experiencing significant financial hardship and am unable to pay on my account (due to *unemployment, disability, divorce, illness, etc.*). This letter is an exercise of my rights as a consumer under federal and state debt collection laws. I am aware that if your organization does not cease and desist attempting to contact me further, I have every right to file a complaint with the attorney general's office, and also with the Federal Trade Commission. If your company does not follow its legal obligations under the Fair Debt Collection Practices Act, I do intend to pursue any and all civil and criminal claims I have against your company for its unlawful acts.

(Insert a description of any harassment tactics the company has used against you.) I would like to use this letter as a warning that I may use telephone-recording devices to document any further phone conversations that we may have in the future.

If any negative information is placed on my credit reports after receipt of this letter, I will then pursue any and all available legal remedies against you and your company.

Sincerely,
(Your Name)
cc: Better Business Bureau
(Your Address)

Credit Card Rating Services

CardTrak, RAM Research, P.O. Box 1700, Frederick, MD 21702. 1-800/344-7714. Publishes list of banks and credit unions offering credit cards with low finance charges, low or no annual fees, and full grace periods. Cost of report is $5, or you may obtain it free online at www.creditcard.com.

Obtaining Your Credit Report

When you are experiencing difficult financial times and have fallen behind on your payments to your creditors, your credit record will show your payment problems. In order to determine how you should handle your credit problems, you should first get a copy of your credit report. This will allow you to see which, if any, of your creditors are reporting your accounts as delinquent. You should also look for any mistakes in the credit report.

Free Credit Report

A new law went into effect in January 2005. The law allows each person to request a free copy of his credit report, one copy from each of three national credit reporting agencies. As of March 2005 there were 96 **imposter sites** on the Internet for requesting your credit report. The best process is to request your credit report by mail to only one of each of the three major credit reporting agencies four months apart; for example, to Experian in April, Equifax in August, and TransUnion in December: Address your mail inquiries to: Annual Credit Report Request Service, P.O. Box 105281, Atlanta, GA 30348-5281

Each credit bureau requires specific information before releasing a report to you, such as your full name, Social Security number, date of birth, and addresses for the last five years. You may also be required to provide additional information.

Some parts of the **Fair and Accurate Transaction Act (FACT Act)** went into effect June 4, 2004. The remainder of the act went into effect December 1, 2004. The FACT Act makes it easier to get a copy of your credit report. The act gives you the right to one free credit report each year, regardless of your circumstances, from Experian, Equifax, and TransUnion. The act requires that credit-card numbers be masked on cash register receipts. It enables identity theft victims to call one credit bureau to place fraud alerts in their credit files, with other bureaus automatically notified. It makes it illegal for a company to ignore a fraud alert. It requires businesses to provide identity theft victims with records of transactions that a thief has generated. It prohibits a bank from sharing medical information about you with its affiliates. It enables consumers to dispute mistakes on their credit reports by approaching the creditor that furnished the information. And it promotes financial literacy.

If you find incorrect information in your credit report, you should send a written dispute to each credit bureau that has reported inaccurate information. The credit bureau must reinvestigate the entry and correct the erroneous information, usually within 30 days of your letter disputing the charges. The creditor who supplied the inaccurate information must also correct their information on you if you can show them that the reported information was not accurate or complete. You can also request delinquent accounts and reference to a Chapter 13 over 7 years old, or Chapter 7 bankruptcy over 10 years old, be deleted from your records by sending a written request to the credit bureaus.

If you dispute information contained in your credit report and the creditor or credit bureau does not correct it after you make a request, you can submit a short statement concerning the charge to the credit bureau to include on your report. The statement cannot be longer than 120 words. You can also notify the credit bureau that you intend to notify the Federal Trade Commission of the discrepancy; this will sometimes result in the disputed information being removed.

Sample Letter to Request a Credit Report

You might want to request a credit report in order to see everything that creditors can see when they check your credit. An updated credit report will also help your records to give you an idea of whom you owe. You may send a letter just like this one to any one of the three credit bureaus listed above. However, in order to receive a free credit report annually from each of the three major credit reporting agencies (Experian, Equifax, and TransUnion), go to www.annualcreditreport.com. I recommend that you alternate your requests spread out over the year, one to Experian in April, one to Equifax in July, and one to TransUnion in December. That way, you have a thorough check throughout the year.

Date: (Today's Date)
To: Annual Credit Report Request Service
P.O. Box 105281
Atlanta, GA 30348-5281

I am requesting a free copy of my annual credit report. I am enclosing a document identifying me by my name and address (*driver's license or utility bill with current address*).
-or-
I am requesting a free credit report because I have been denied credit, insurance, employment or a rental dwelling because of information supplied by the credit bureau. Attached is a denial letter.
-or-
I am requesting a free credit report because I have recently experienced identity theft.
-or-
I am requesting a free credit report because I am currently unemployed and seeking employment.

Please send me a copy of my credit report to:

Full Name: (*your name*)
Date of Birth: (*your date of birth*)
Social Security Number: (*social security #*)
Spouse's Name: (*spouse's name*)
Telephone Number: (*telephone number*)
Current Address: (*current address*)
Dates at Current Address: (*dates at address*)
(*List previous addresses and dates to cover a five-year period*)
Thank you for your attention to this matter.

Sincerely,
(*Your name*)

How to Avoid Being Sued; Options for Handling Problem Debt

- Loan Consolidation
- Payment Agreements
- Judgment Proof Letter
- Consumer Credit Counselors
- Bankruptcy

Loan Consolidation

If your credit history allows you to qualify, you can take out a large loan to pay off your smaller debts. The advantage is that you consolidate your debts into one payment. The disadvantage is that you may incur larger finance charges. Extreme caution should be used as it may affect your future ability to discharge the debt in bankruptcy. To consolidate your loans, contact the Direct Loan Service Center at 1-800-848-0982.

Payment Agreements

Unless you think that you do not owe any money to your creditor, or cannot pay any amount in the near future, it is probably best for you to arrange an agreement with the debt collector. The debt collector may allow you to make a lump sum payment or partial payments until you pay your bill. Usually a creditor or collection agency is more interested in receiving payment rather than starting a lawsuit or continuing collection activities. The more time they spend trying to collect your debt, the more money it costs them. Remember, however, that a debt collector does not have to accept a payment plan.

Negotiating Tips

- **Start by offering to pay a portion of the original debt.** Creditors will sometimes accept as little as one-third of the debt.

- **Decide beforehand the most you can pay, and don't go any higher than you can afford.** Making promises you can't keep will start the whole process all over again.

- **Make sure any agreement you make is in writing.** Send your agreement by mail, and request that the debt collector respond to your agreement in writing.

- **If you are seriously considering bankruptcy, say so.**

- **Never disclose where you work or bank.** If you do make a payment, don't send a check from your own bank! Send a money order.

Use the following sample letter as a guide in writing to your creditor arranging a settlement agreement. You should only send this letter if you are willing and able to negotiate a settlement. Do not offer to pay more than you can. Rewrite the letter as necessary to fit your situation. Keep a copy of this letter and all communication with your creditor.

Date: Today's Date
To: Name and Address of Creditor or Collection Agency
From: Your Name
RE: Your Account Number

Dear (Name of Creditor or Collection Agency):
This letter is to inform you that due to (*unemployment, illness, disability, divorce, or other*), I am experiencing significant financial hardship and am unable to pay on my account as obligated. I propose the following settlement agreement:

I offer to pay $___ a month for ___ months to satisfy my obligation to you. (Or: I offer to pay a lump sum amount of $___ to satisfy my obligation to you.) This is all that I can pay due to my financial situation, and I do not foresee my situation improving in the near future.

Please respond by mail to my offer. Please cease all communication by phone regarding this matter.

Thank you for your understanding,

Sincerely,
(*Your Signature*)

Judgment Proof Letter

You cannot afford a payment agreement and are "judgment proof." You are judgment proof if you receive government benefits such as AFDC, Social Security, or MediCal, own no – or have little equity in – real estate, and have limited personal property.

A powerful weapon is explaining to your creditor that you are judgment proof. This means that your property is "exempt." It can not be taken by your creditors to pay what you owe them even if you have a court judgment against you, because you do not have enough money or assets to pay your creditor anything.

To avoid a lawsuit, write to your creditors a letter explaining that you are judgment proof and cannot pay the debt. However, if your creditor doesn't sue you within a certain amount of time, they can never sue you. And once they have a judgment against you, it's good for 10 years. Since they know that you may be in a different financial situation in 10 years, they may want to win a judgment against you now with hopes of getting the money later. Telling them you are judgment proof now may make them go away, but you can't count on it.

If you are judgment proof and do not foresee your situation changing, you may want to send the following letter. You should only send this letter if you are being harassed and want creditors to stop contacting you. This letter may result in a lawsuit and judgment against you. If your financial situation changes within 10 years of receiving a judgment and you are able to pay your debt, the creditor has a right to collect the money you owe.

Date: Today's Date

To: Name and Address of Creditor or Collection Agency
From: Your Name
RE: Your Account Number

Dear (Name of Creditor or Collection Agency):
This letter is to inform you that due to (*unemployment, illness, disability, divorce, or other*), I am experiencing significant financial hardship and am unable to pay on my account as obligated. I am familiar with state law and I know that I am "Judgment Proof." My only source of income is (*Unemployment/Social Security/Disability/Aid to Families with Dependent Children*). Accordingly, under 15 U.S.C. section 1692c(c), this is my formal request to you to cease all further communication with me for the reasons specifically set forth in the law.

Sincerely,
(*Your Signature*)

Consumer Credit Counselors

Consumer Credit Counseling Service is an organization that provides debt counseling and possible mortgage solutions if you are facing foreclosure on your home or are in financial straits. They will not advise you on your legal defense, help you set up a budget and teach you basic money management principles. They work with your creditors to arrange a debt repayment plan that you can afford. You make monthly deposits to the CCCS office, and they distribute the money to your creditors. If you have more than one creditor and need help developing a workable repayment schedule, you may want to contact CCCS. You do have to pay a nominal amount for this service, however.

Check the Yellow Pages of your telephone book for the phone number of the local Consumer Credit Counselors or call 1-800-750-2227.

Considering Bankruptcy

Bankruptcy may be used as a protection from your creditors when you are consistently unable to meet your monthly bills. Bankruptcy should be considered only when you have something to lose if you are sued, such as wages or property or if things are starting to look up for you. **If you are judgment proof, you should not consider bankruptcy.**

Depending on the type of bankruptcy you choose and your personal situation, bankruptcy may allow you to keep some or all of your assets, including your home and car. You may have to give up some of your property in order to pay off your debts. Property you can keep, depending on your situation, may include:

- Your home
- Car
- Furniture
- Salary
- Future earnings
- Life insurance
- Tools of your trade

Bankruptcy stays on your credit for 10 years, which will make it difficult, but not impossible, to get credit in the future. Also, you cannot get federally insured loans during this period. The bankruptcy-filing fee is over $150, and is not waivable.

Bankruptcy does not cancel all of your debts. You still must pay:

- Secured debts
- Any creditors you do not list when you file for bankruptcy
- Most income taxes and penalties for the last three years
- Most student loans
- Child and spousal support
- Any money you owe if you were sued for drunk driving or other intentional injury you caused to another's person or property
- Debts obtained through fraud

Current Bankruptcy Law

The New Bankruptcy Laws took effect in 2005. The major intent of bankruptcy reform is to require people who can afford to make some payments towards their debt to make these payments, while still affording them the right to have the rest of their debt erased. These people must file Chapter 13.

Means Test: This will identify debtors who have the financial capacity to pay some money to their creditors. The test will work as follows:

- **Test 1:** Is the family earning above the median income for their state? If the answer is "No," Chapter 7 can be filed.

- **Test 2:** If the answer is "Yes" to Test 1, do you have excess monthly income of more than $166.66/month to pay $10,000 of debt over five years? If the answer is "No," you must answer another question. If "Yes," Chapter 7 cannot be filed but Chapter 13 may be filed.

- **Test 3:** If the answer is "No" to Test 2, do you have excess income of greater than $100/month to pay over the next 60 months at least 25 percent of your unsecured debt? If the answer is "No," you can file Chapter 7. If "Yes," Chapter 7 cannot be filed but Chapter 13 may be filed.

- **Proof of Income:** Debtors filing Chapter 7 or Chapter 13 bankruptcy must provide to the trustee, at least seven days prior to the 341 meeting, a copy of a tax return or transcript of a tax return, for the period for which the return was most recently due.

- **State Exemptions:** You cannot use the exemptions in your state of residence unless you have lived there at least two years.

- **Homesteads:** This went into effect as soon as the bill was signed by the president. The exemption is limited to $125,000 if the property was acquired within the previous 1,215 days (3.3 years). The cap is not applicable to any interest transferred from a debtor's previous principal residence which was acquired prior to the beginning of the 1,215-day period. The value of the exemption is reduced by any addition to the value brought about on account of a disposition of nonexempt property made by the debtor during the 10 years prior to the bankruptcy filing.

- **Counseling:** You must have finished counseling within the last six months before you can file bankruptcy.

- **Child Support and Alimony:** These debts would go from a priority of 7th to 1st.

- **Tithing:** Up to 15 percent of your income can be given to charity. This is seen by some as a loophole allowing people who may be just over the threshold of having to file Chapter 13 to drop down low enough to file Chapter 7.

- **Pension Plans:** Employee contributions to ERISA qualified retirement plans, deferred compensation plans, tax-deferred annuities, and health insurance plans are exempt from seizure.

- **Education Funds:** Funds placed in an educational retirement account or qualified state funds placed in an educational retirement account or qualified state tuition programs at least 365 days prior to a bankruptcy filing, within the limits established by the Internal Revenue Code, and for the benefit of a child or grandchild of the debtor, are excluded from the debtor's estate, with a $5,000 limit on funds contributed between one and two years before the filing.

Being Sued – The Lawsuit Process

If your creditor decides to sue, you need to understand the process so that you can protect yourself and your property. If you are being sued in Small Claims Court, the process is different that of Municipal or Superior Court. Please contact the Small Claims Advisory Clinic to be advised as to what to do. If you are being sued in Municipal or Superior Court, the following information should help you understand the process and steps you should take to defend yourself in court.

- **The Summons and the Complaint.** The creditor will let you know that they are suing you by a process called a service of a summons and complaint. This set of papers will tell you who is suing you, how much money they want, which court you will be in, and who the opposing attorney is.

- **You Must File an Answer.** You have 30 days from the day you were served to file an answer with the court or your creditor will file a default judgment against you. This means that you lose automatically. Your answer can be filed by using a form available at the courthouse from the court clerk or from the Voluntary Legal Services Program's Debt Collection Defense Clinic. You must also serve and file a Proof of Service form with the answer, which tells the court that you served the opposing party with a copy of your answer. The Proof of Service form is also available from the court clerk or the clinic.

- **Defenses.** If you have a defense to the creditor's demand for payment or you don't think you owe the money, you will put that information in your answer. Possible defenses are:

    - The creditor has been paid.
    - The good purchased was defective or the service was not performed.
    - The **statute of limitation** has passed. meaning the debt cannot be collected because the creditor waited too long to file the suit.
    - The contract you entered into is "unconscionable." The terms of the contract or the creditor's actions in getting your promise to pay were so outrageous that they would shock the average person.
    - **Fraud or duress.** The seller lied to you or threatened you so that you would enter into the contract.
    - **Incapacity.** You were too young when you entered into the contract or mentally incapable of understanding the contract and cannot be held responsible for the debt.
    - **Mistake.** A mistake in the contract makes it unenforceable.
    - **Statute of frauds.** Under certain conditions oral contracts are no good. Many contracts must be in writing.

    This is not a complete list of defenses. If you think you may have a defense, you should speak to a lawyer.

- **Negotiating a Settlement.** You may want to try again to negotiate an alternative settlement. A settlement is better than a judgment entered against you. But be sure to answer the complaint, no matter what. This will buy you more time and will insure that you do not lose automatically.

- **Trial.** After you file your answer, you will be given a court date, usually 45-60 days later. The judge will decide whether or not your case is appropriate for arbitration. If you are ordered to arbitration, you must appear at the arbitration and present your case to the arbitrator. If the judge does not feel your case should be arbitrated, you will have another court appearance approximately 30 days later to pick a trial date. Your trial will be scheduled about 3-6 months after your court appearance to pick the trial date. At the trial date, you must appear on time at the department to which you have been assigned or the creditor will win the case.

- **If You Lose the Lawsuit.** If you cannot settle and your creditor can prove that you owe money, the court will enter a judgment against you. At this point you are a **judgment debtor,** and your creditor is a **judgment creditor.** In practical terms, this means your creditor can now enforce the judgment by trying to take your assets.

- **After the Judgment – Enforcement.** If the lawsuit demanded money and you did not pay what the judge ordered you to pay, something you own can be attached, or taken. Once judgment is entered against you, the judgment creditor will go to the Sheriff's department to enforce the judgment. The Sheriff's department will notify you that the judgment creditor has filed for enforcement of the debt.

- **A Judgment Creditor May Try to Enforce the Judgment in the Following Ways:**
    - **Attachment of your bank account.** This means that the creditor can take money out of your bank account. If this happens, you will receive notice and can ask the court to return the money.
    - **Wage garnishment.** The law allows your employer to withhold up to 25 percent of your net wages to pay your debt. Your net wages are what you take home after any mandatory reductions, such as taxes. The sheriff contacts your employer, who then notifies you of the garnishment.
    - **Attachment of personal property.** A car, for example, may be attached and sold to satisfy the debt.
    - **Lien on real property.** This means that your house or land cannot be sold or refinanced until you pay off your creditor. In some cases it can be sold at auction to pay the debt.

- **Order of Examination.** The judgment creditor may ask the court to order you to appear for an examination. You must either appear, or notify the court in writing if you cannot make your date. At the examination, you will be asked about assets, wages, and bank accounts that may be attached to satisfy your debt. You must answer these questions.

- **Protecting Your Property If You Are Judgment Proof: Claim of Exemption.** When you receive notice of an attachment, you have 10 days to file a claim of exemption, which protects some of your property. Your assets may be judgment proof, as mentioned earlier. The judgment creditor cannot take the following away from you:
    - Wages that are used for necessities of life, such as rent, food, child care, clothing. This may mean that the judgment creditor cannot attach any of your wages.
    - A car or other motor vehicles to the value of $1,900.
    - Income from AFDC, SSI, Workers Compensation, Veterans benefits, life insurance, disability, retirement and pension.

- Ordinary and reasonably necessary household furnishings.
- Jewelry and art not to exceed $5,000.
- Property necessary to be used in trade or profession, up to $5,000.
- Direct deposit account for SSI benefits, $2,000 or $3,000 if married.
- Life insurance benefits on which you can borrow up to $8,000.
- Up to $1,000 in an inmate's trust account.
- A cemetery plot.
- Paid wages, 75% of your wages for the last 30 days.

This is not a complete list. Also, if you bought the property on credit or pledged it for a loan, such as for a car or furnishings, then the creditor does have the right to take it away.

Once you have filed the exemption, the creditor has 10 days to contest your exemption and the matter is set for hearing. You **must** go to the hearing. If you do not, the exemption will be denied. When you go to the hearing you will have to prove that you are entitled to the exemptions that you are claiming. After hearing both sides, the court will allow your exemptions, deny them, or compromise somewhere in between.

Remember: If your situation changes and you become able to pay the debt, you will have to pay. The creditor's judgment is good for 10 years.

Length of Time Negative Information Stays on Credit Report

1. **Collection Accounts, Charge-offs, and Past-Due Accounts:** 7 years from the date of occurrence (when the account became negative).

2. **Tax Liens (Unpaid):** 7 years from date filed (Experian and Equifax); indefinitely on TransUnion (RCA).

3. **Tax Liens Released (Paid):** 7 years from the date filed; TransUnion (RCA) is 7 years from date paid.

4. **Judgments:** If paid, 7 years from the date filed. If not paid, 10 years and can be renewed twice.

5. **Bankruptcy Chapter 7, 11, 12:** 10 years from date filed.

6. **Bankruptcy Chapter 13:** If completed, 7 years from date filed. If not completed, 10 years from date filed. Once you file, if you change your mind and choose not to do the bankruptcy, it remains on the report for 10 years.

7. **Federally Insured Student Loans:** 7 years from the date the loan was assigned to the government for repayment, or, if the account was never reported to the bureau before, 7 years from the date the government first reports the default to the credit bureau.

Defaulted Student Loans

Your Options

- Student loan default blots your credit record and may follow you for 7 years or longer – time incarcerated does not count in purging it from your credit report!
- Failure to repay a student loan may result in your school, lender, state, and federal government taking action against you to recover this money. You can even be sued. The lender may:

    1. Attach your tax returns.
    2. Attach your wages. You will have 30 days to respond to this notice. Respond immediately by negotiating with the lender an amount that you can afford.
    3. You may negotiate a payment plan. Failure to repay may affect your ability to get an auto loan or to obtain other student loans and grants. To negotiate a payment plan, call 1-800-621-3115 or the Federal Student Aid Information Center at 1-800-433-3243.

Recommended Spending Levels

The following are only **recommended** spending levels. You may need to adjust them, depending on various categories of living expenditures.

- Live on 60 percent of your monthly gross income.
- Put 10 percent into savings.
- Put 20 percent into taxes (this figure may vary depending on your income).
- Donate 10 percent to a church or charity, or pay off credit cards by accelerating payments, or invest in a retirement fund such as an IRA.

Installment Payments: How Much is Too Much?

- Excluding mortgage or rent, if your monthly installment payments to businesses like Sears, JC Penney, or Macy's are over 15 percent of your gross monthly income, you are using too much credit. Gross income is your earnings, while net income is your take-home pay.
- If your monthly installment payments reach 20 percent or more, you are in serious trouble and may be headed for a Chapter 13 or 7 bankruptcy.

Children's Primer on Economic Success

Encourage your daughter (or son) to learn about business and become economically independent. *Debt-Proof Your Kids* by Mary Hunt offers ways a parent can help children to become economically literate.

There are so many books about kids and money. Each one comes from a little different approach. In *Debt-Proof Your Kids*, Mary Hunt tells how they taught their kids to handle money. They have a unique approach that gradually increases the financial responsibility each year until the child finally graduates from the program and is on his or her own financially. She and her husband wanted to make sure that their kids made their financial mistakes while they were still small and not life changing.

When each of their boys entered 6th grade, they were given a monthly salary. This salary consisted of monies that their parents typically handed out to them throughout the year for items such as video games, snacks, food away from home, school lunches, etc. They were given the salary at the beginning of each month and would not be given any kind of loan or bailout during the month. There were guidelines that they had to follow regarding giving and saving. In regards to spending, they were allowed to spend the money as they desired (except on items forbidden because of moral issues) with the understanding that it had to last them the entire month. The parents' job was to teach them basic financial principles, then sit back and let the boys learn through their experiences. Mary Hunt explains that one of the hardest things to do was to keep their mouths shut and let the boys make mistakes. She said that by doing that, they eliminated many of the typical battles that occur between parents and teenagers.

Each year the salary and responsibilities would increase. They were very careful to provide enough money for the kids to be able to cover the expenses that they were responsible for, but not without careful money management. They couldn't live a lavish lifestyle. Tough choices had to be made (just as we have to make them every day). Through this system, they were able to watch their kids learn important lessons before they were adults.

The Amazing Kid Entrepreneur, by Zohra Sarwari is about a normal kid, named Yasmine. Yasmine is taught by her mother about how money is earned at the age of 6. As she learns about the fundamentals of money, and how she can make it, she never realizes what she can achieve. Going to school, holding a job, and trying to make her dream come true has its obstacles. Can 6-year old Yasmine understand the difficulties and power in being able to achieve her dreams? And can Yasmine make it? Every dream begins with an idea, every idea leads to action, and every action leads to achieving a goal. For more than a decade, Zohra Sarwari has inspired youth of all ages as a business and life coach. Currently, she is focused on grooming her own children into becoming entrepreneurs with a lofty goal of earning 1 million dollars before the age of 18. As a humanitarian, Zohra is passionate about helping others view the world through a new lens and recognize their own potential for greatness. As a leader, Zohra teaches by example and inspires individuals to "believe and they shall achieve," and helps people turn obstacles into energy and focus. Zohra is committed to teaching the formula of success, one person at a time.) (Suggestion: to demonstrate investment growth to a child, put a checkerboard on a table with a bag of small-grain rice. Put one grain of rice on the first square, doubling the number for each successive square, thus demonstrating rapid growth of a savings fund at the end, not the beginning, of the investment period. The total grains of rice would be about 18×10^{18}. That would be the number 18 followed by 18 zeroes!)

Chapter 12

Recovery, Relapse Prevention, and Search for Meaning

"It is never too late to become what you might have been."
– George Eliot

Recovery of Meaning

A recovery of meaning is the ultimate avenue to the recovery of health and relapse prevention. If we were really dominated by a desire for pleasure, there would be little hope we would suspend the pleasures of perpetual intoxication for the agony of sobriety. If we were really dominated by desire for power, there would be little expectation that the artificially empowered drunkard would yield to the weaker state of sobriety. It is in terms of a regained sense of meaning and purpose that the pain and frustration of sobriety are risked by the addict or alcoholic as a viable option for life. Meaning is the ultimate drive pulling mankind toward his meaning potential and purpose. When life has no meaning, it becomes empty. We live in what Viktor Frankl calls an existential vacuum. It is a state of inertia, boredom, and apathy experienced by many. If this state persists, it progresses into existential frustration, and eventually becomes a spiritual neurosis. We try to fill the existential vacuum with drugs, violence, also with food, over-work, sports, etc., yet remain unfulfilled. Every day we have many possibilities from which to choose within our area of freedom. We must choose the most responsible option; make the best choice, not only for ourselves, but also the people around us then happiness and meaning fulfillment will ensue.

Relapse is a Response

Relapse is not generally triggered by physical cravings. Relapse is a response to stress, anxiety, fear, anger, frustration, depression, social pressure to use, or interpersonal conflicts. How we interpret the events of our lives controls the intensity and frequency of our feelings of anxiety, fear, anger, frustration, or depression. Even if we can't change a situation or circumstance, we can still choose our attitude toward a condition; this is often a self-transcending way of finding meaning, especially in unavoidable suffering. A person coming out of an otherwise successful rehabilitation may ask of him or herself, "Ok, so I got clean… Now what?" Leaving this question unanswered seems to be an invitation to relapse. While incentive-based motivations can help a person initiate a change, a meaning-based motivation may assure the maintenance of clean and sober gains. Consequently, we are invited to start the recovery process by taking a look **beyond** the recovery, **beyond** the myopia of "getting back on track," **towards** the destination of the life-track. This is accomplished by priming our consciousness with the "meaning of life" questions, i.e. existential and philosophical questions that allow us to broaden our motivational search from short-lived, tactical, and often cliché motivations to person-specific, meaning-centered motivations that serve as a buffer against the turbulence of change.

Interpreting Events and Managing Conflicts

Interpreting events has an effect on our mental health and ability and manage conflicts with others. If there were no conflict we could never evaluate the importance of each others concerns. Conflict is good because it provides an opportunity for fulfilling values, and this potential for values fulfillment carries the **meaning** of the situation! However, we can learn to manage and change how we interpret, respond, and feel about events. Interpersonal conflicts are increased or decreased by the actions we take based on our interpretations, and our emotions that result from our interpretations of events. We can increase our skills in interpreting the events and manage interpersonal conflicts in our lives more accurately with practice.

Negative Thoughts

When we are feeling upset we think negative thoughts; over 87 percent of all self talk tends to be negative. If we feel sad or depressed, we may think 'everything is hopeless; I am a loser; I will never feel good again.' If we feel anxious and panicky, we may think, 'What if I lose control or crack up?' During an argument with our parole or probation officer, we may tell ourselves, 'That SOB! What a jerk! S/he never really cared for my success!' Thinking pessimistically about ourselves and our world leads to despair. Negative thoughts can be exaggerated, distorted and illogical yet they are deceptively realistic, so we believe things are really as bad as we think they are. We all succumb at times to feelings of doubt and despair.

It is not the actual events but our interpretations that result in mood changes. The world is a series of positive, neutral, and negative events – loss of a job; divorce; homeless; loss of a loved one. We interpret the events with a series of thoughts in the form of internal dialogue. Our feelings are created by our thoughts and not the actual events. The major key to understanding our moods is our thoughts. Our emotions result entirely from the way we look at things. It is a neurological fact that before we can experience any event, we must process it with our mind and give it meaning.

Interpretation of Events

We must always check the accuracy of our interpretation of events. If our understanding of what is happening is accurate, our emotions will be a valid response. If our perception is distorted, our emotional response will be abnormal and extreme.

Thoughts Create Emotions

Our thoughts create our emotions. Unpleasant feelings indicate that we are thinking something negative and believing it. Our emotions follow our thoughts as surely as a puppy follows its master. But the fact that a puppy follows faithfully along does not prove its master knows where s/he is going. If we are still being hurt by an event that happened to us at age twelve, it is the thought that is hurting us now.

Thoughts Lead to Action or Inaction

Self-defeating thoughts lead to self-defeating actions, which lead to isolation and un-motivated state of paralysis. Result, we feel tired, bored, discouraged, guilty, helpless, and overwhelmed. Self-defeating negative thoughts make us feel miserable. Painful emotions in turn convince us that our distorted, pessimistic thoughts are actually val-id. Self-defeating thoughts and actions reinforce each other in a circular manner, ever downward. The unpleasant consequences of doing nothing make our problems even worse. Negative distorted thoughts lead to inaction and less action. Action comes first. Action is followed by motivation. If the motivation is positive, it is followed by more action, which increases the motivation to do more. Your reading this guide was an action. Whether you take more action and become more motivated depends on how you interpret reading this chapter. Thoughts, such as, 'This will not help; no hope. This author does not know what s/he is saying. I always relapse. I do not need to change,' lead to the lethargy cycle (of doing nothing) and less action and...

Being Responsible for our Thoughts

What happens now depends significantly on you. You alone are responsible for your thoughts, actions, and feelings. Thoughts lead to emotions and to interpretation. Accu-rate thoughts, such as, 'This chapter on relapse, recovery, and search for meaning has reliable information. I can make friends who do not use drugs or alcohol. I can help myself to learn something helpful to me. I have the defiant power of the human spirit to recover and not relapse. I am tired of using. I am worried,' leads to learning; leads to actions; then, more motivation; then more action...

Realistic and Distorted Thinking

Realistic problems can lead to realistic responses – family member dies; sadness results; life, not death, is celebrated. Valid thoughts create emotions that add depth to our life. Emotions based on distortion create feelings of fear, anger, frustration, hopelessness, and self pity. Distorted or exaggerated thinking is ultimately self-defeating. A common example of distorted thinking is called 'all or nothing thinking.' 'black or white think-ing.' distorted thinking can become an automatic interpretation of all events in our life.

Examples of all or nothing thinking when used as automatic filters are, 'This pro-gram is no good and I will never get any better. People should never disagree with me; they should respect my views. I should always have something to say. My world should be the way I want it to be and it never is. I will always have to be afraid that I will use. No one can truly understand me. I have a right to be sad or angry with the people around me. My life is hell.' Relapse is inevitable. Use of drugs or alcohol is justified, 'I got laid off again. It is all management's fault. They are incompetent jerks. I am no good. I want to drink (use).' The emotions are sadness, shame, anger and bitterness.

The same event can result in different interpretations and emotions, 'I got laid off. That was really tough, but I kept my coo and my head held high. I am going to miss the management, my co-workers, and the steady income. I feel pride and sadness. I will spend more time in the evenings playing with my children, exercising, and enrolling in college.'

Problems are Opportunities

Think of a negative event that has been bugging you for a long time – Dropping out of school; being fired; getting stood up; getting divorced; death of a loved one. All of these events are examples of memories or 'problems' we may hold onto for years. Using a worksheets, write a brief description of an event that whenever you think of it, you feel sad, angry, anxious, ashamed, depressed, worried.

When you feel negative, can you change the way you feel? Take five minutes to write your answers to the following questions.

1. How long have I been feeling this way?
2. Am I doing something constructive about the problem or am I simply brooding and avoiding it?
3. Are my thoughts and feelings realistic?
4. Am I making myself unhappy about a problem that is beyond my control?
5. Am I avoiding a problem and denyi9ng that I am really upset about it?
6. Are my expectations for the world realistic?
7. Are my expectations for myself realistic?
8. Am I feeling hopeless?
9. Am I experiencing a loss of self esteem?
10. Am I pursuing my real meaning potential or letting others roll the dice?

Deciding when we are tired of just feeling bad about an event or problem is all up to us. Taking action and changing our attitude and the way we feel about an event requires the coping skills taught in Logotherapy, Rational Emotive Therapy, 12-Steps, and other recovery programs. (Refer to www.usdrugrehabcenters.com for drug rehab centers, alcohol treatment centers, recovery homes, support groups, other addiction services, drug rehabilitation resources, drug rehab information, and drug rehab blog. These are listed by state.)

Developing Skills Requires Active Participation

Developing skills requires participation, and long-term repetition. We need to be an active participant in the skills training process and address our real problems. The more passive we are, the less likely we will use the new skills when we leave a program. Homework activities are compulsory so we become motivated through action rather than waiting for a feeling to move us to action. Nobody becomes good at a skill by simply watching others perform it. Good, better, best, never let it rest until your good is better, and your better is...well, better. On our way to recovery and not relapsing, we can begin fulfilling our meaning potential, one day at a time.

Daily Recovery Training

All learning starts with information being stored in our brain. When we learn anything, we first use current brain connections to store information. After brief and repeated periods of practice, we begin to strengthen existing brain synapse connections. Practice makes for improvement, not perfection. These connections are rapidly reversed and memory of the learning fades when learning is not practiced. To truly master new skills we need continued practice. Maintaining improvement and making a recovery skill permanent requires the slow steady work that forms new connections. Sustained practice solidifies learning because it goes beyond strengthening existing neuronal connections in the brain. It actually creates new neuronal connections and synapses. More permanent change takes up to six months of training. Daily recovery training leads to dramatic short term changes and continued training leads to more permanent changes and less chance to relapse. Coping skills require repetition and practice just like any skill. Any musical skill must be practiced daily over a lifetime to be maintained. So too must coping skills be practiced continuously.

Logotherapy

Logotherapy is useful because it can be combined with any other form of drug and alcohol therapy. It is also prophylactic in preventing relapse. Addicts are pushed to seek refuge in narcotics and alcohol by inner conflicts over values, behavior, and conscience. They turn to narcotics to disassociate from nature, their former self, and from anyone not in the drug culture. They are experiencing spiritual chaos; intense guilt for having compromised truth, failed to combat injustice, stolen from and exploited friends and family, and not realized their meaning potential. Logotherapy makes available that 'spiritual substitute' for alcohol and drugs; the spiritual reality for which alcohol and drugs became a substitute.

Logotherapy has been used as an alternative to the 12-step program for more than fifty years. In Logotherapy, or "health through meaning," emphasis is given to the absence in the "will to meaning." When we lack a will to meaning, noted Viktor Frankl, we generally seek to fill the existential vacuum with a "will to pleasure," often leading to addictions, or a "will to power," often leading to aggression or violence. Frankl repeatedly emphasized the importance of meaning as essential for the health of the body, mind, and spirit. He believed that the key to a positive view of life is awareness that life has meaning under all circumstances, and that we have the capacity to find meaning in our life "experientially, creatively, and attitudinally." We can rise above ill health and blows of fate if we can see meaning in our existence. Logotherapy helps people say yes to life, whether the suffering they experience comes from difficult human relationships, job dissatisfaction, life-altering illness, survivor's guilt, or death of a loved one, or from self-made problems such as hypochondria or an overwhelming hunger for pleasure, power and prosperity.

Logotherapy was introduced to incarcerated individuals about fifty years ago as a short-term project. The program aimed at giving incarcerated individuals a purpose and direction in life, and at helping them acquire the knowledge needed to pursue a new direction during and after their prison experience. The individuals, who participated in the project learned to see that their very experiences as convicted criminals gave them a unique opportunity to help others, thus turning their liabilities into assets society could use. The recidivism rate for those who completed the program prior to parole was only 5.5 percent. Furthermore, when utilized as an addictions treatment program, it was found to be four times as effective as any other addictions program.

Shared Meaning Exercises

1. Imagine yourself holding your infant child or partner while at the same time thinking how precarious life is. When you glance down at your child or partner's sleeping face, think about how soon s/he may die. At that moment, overwhelmed by your love for her/him, aware of the very fact that your child or partner and you have only a very short time together makes love more than just a familial arrangement. When you fully realize that everyone is destined to die, every moment you waste is wasted forever. Now, contemplate the life that you have had with this person and write about the meaningful times you have shared.

2. Being human being means being creative. When creativity is in retreat, we feel arid and unmoved. The ebb and the flow in the creative process operate at various times, in varying degrees. Dry times, particularly during incarceration can be disappointing, even alarming, especially if our livelihood is depending upon it. But there are many tools and techniques that help to ease those shades off. The creative spirit does not leave. It simply goes into retreat. And when we find the opening again, it returns in a way that feels at once familiar and new. Creative expression is in a perpetual, evolutionary stage. When it returns, we experience ourselves and our world just a bit more fully than before. A poet must write. A musician must perform. A mechanic must be mechanical. Our vocation is our calling. When we are not involved in it, we feel that existential vacuum. Think of a creative endeavor that makes your life meaningful. Devote at least one hour each week to what you enjoy and share it with another as a mentor, such as your child or partner.

3. Ernest Hemingway says, "The world breaks everyone and afterward many are strong in the broken places." Former Senator Max Cleland lost both legs and an arm in Vietnam. He recovered and went on to become a U.S. Senator, a motivational speaker, and writer. Liz Murray grew up in a dysfunctional family with addicted parents, homeless until she was 19, never having attended school until she was 17. She often survived living off food found in garbage bins. Her mother died from AIDS. Despite the hardships, she went on to complete her high school education and attended Harvard University on a four-year, full scholarship. Jerry Long, a promising baseball player at age 17, broke his neck and became a

quadriplegic. Nine years later he graduated with a doctorate in psychology. He noted that "the accident broke my neck. It did not break me."

When we experience a flat tire on the highway, we can be depressed or give thanks that the other three tires are still inflated. Viktor Frankl "insists meaning is available in spite of – nay, even through suffering, provided...that the suffering is unavoidable. If it is avoidable, the meaningful thing to do is to remove its cause, for unnecessary suffering is masochistic rather than heroic. If, on the other hand, one cannot change a situation that causes his suffering, he can still choose his attitude. Jerry Long had not...chosen to break his neck, but he did decide not to let himself be broken by what had happened to him." You have possibly experienced brokenness throughout your life, but each was undoubtedly followed by spiritually uplifting events. Take time to note those facts.

Preventing Relapse

Many relapse because they don't understand the process and what to do to prevent it. Appropriate action on your part and the people in your life can prevent or interrupt the relapse syndrome before consequences become tragic. The affirmation steps are:

1. **Stabilization -** "I can and must get back in control of myself and my behavior one day at a time."

2. **Assessment -** "I can and must figure out, with the help of others, what is causing my relapse episodes."

3. **Education -** "I can and must learn about the process of my relapse and how to prevent it one day at a time."

4. **Warning Sign Identification -** "I must identify the warning signs that tell me I'm in trouble with my sobriety, criminal behavior, or mental health."

5. **Warning Sign Management -** "On a daily basis I can and must have concrete plans for preventing and stopping behavior associated with warning signs of relapse."

6. **Inventory Training -** "I must consciously do an inventory twice daily so I can notice the first signs of trouble and correct the problems before they get out of hand."

7. **Review of the Recovery Program -** "I must review my current program regularly to be sure there is help in coping with my warning signs of relapse."

8. **Involvement of Others -** "I can and must ask others to help me stay sober, mentally healthy, and prosocial by telling them about my warning signs and asking for feedback if they see any developing."

A final note on addiction treatment: The type of addiction treatment may not matter as much as whether sufficient treatment has been provided. The **strongest predictors** of positive outcome are days in treatment and number of sessions in treatment. Do not assume that there is a quick fix to drug addiction. The cells of an addict's body have been changed, altered. It will take time to recover.

Drug Treatment

A chemically dependent alcoholic has no "freedom" about the dependency but **is free**, after detoxification, to decide whether or not to take that first, fateful drink. The same thing applies to those addicted to other drugs, legal or illegal. In 2005 Merck marketed acamprosate **(Campral)** to battle alcoholism for the person who has stopped drinking. The drug has been available in Europe for about 15 years. It is the first anti-relapse medication that works to normalize alcohol-induced changes in the brain functions of alcoholics after they stop drinking and to reduce alcohol cravings. People take the drug for as long as a year after they abstain from alcohol.

Other drug-treatment options for people trying to end alcohol dependence are: **Antabuse** (makes people violently ill if they drink while on the medication) and **ReVia** (acts on opioid receptors in the brain to help reduce alcohol cravings for people currently drinking) and is not recommended for people with hepatitis or liver diseases).

Depression

A person suffering from a biologically caused depression that comes and goes without apparent reason has no way to fight the unavoidable, oncoming attack except by taking medication to diminish the intensity of the depression. But he or she is free to lead a meaningful life during periods of normalcy between depressions.

Elderly people cannot always avoid the consequences of the aging process – loss of hearing, deterioration of sight, loss of friends who die, forced retirement, and deteriorating mobility, for example. But they can to use their assets, which include experience and wisdom.

True Freedom

True freedom comes about one day at a time. It comes from discovering that all experiences, encounters with others, including loves, benefit you in some unique way. Failing to learn the unique lessons of your life may lead to a path of the "sui-circle bird," which flies in circles that become smaller and smaller, eventually flying up its own back side in self-destruction – relapse, recidivism, bankruptcy, underemployment, divorce, etc. The avenues toward freedom are discovered by pursuing and improving your creative abilities, doing thingsfor others (volunteer), and taking on an attitude of thankfulness for those events over which you have no control.

Life is Not Fair

Life is not fair. You discovered that when your parents divorced and fought over you as though you were a possession. You learned that life was not fair when you were abused as a child, when you grew up in the home of a physically and/or emotionally absent parent, and when you were a victim of acts of violence or witnessed the death of a loved one. Every person has experienced, is experiencing, or will experience pain, guilt, and – eventually – death. But life is worth living because there is somebody who truly cares for you, even though you may not know his/her name or be able to see him/her.

Delancey Street Foundation

- San Francisco: 600 Embarcadero San Francisco, CA 94107, Tel. 415-512-5104
- Los Angeles: 400 N. Vermont Ave, Los Angeles, CA 90004, Tel. 323-644-4122
- New Mexico: P.O. Box 1240, San Juan Pueblo, NM 87566, Tel. 505-852-4291 x304
- North Carolina: 811 N. Elm St, Greensboro, NC 27401, Tel. 336-379-8477
- New York: 100 Turk Hill Road, Brewster, New York 10509, Tel. 845-278-6181 x205

Chapter 13

Resource Directory for the Pre-Paroled

*Remember that there is nothing
permanent in life but change.*

A.A./N.A. Directory
- www.aa.org, www.na.org

Adult Basic Education
- Locate basic skill, ESL and GED programs in your area: www.literacydirectory.org and www.esl.com
- Free sample GED tests online: www.acenet.edu or www.testprepreview.com
- Locate GED testing centers: www.acenet.edu or call 1-800-626-9433
- Locate vocational programs: www.careerinfonet.org

Community-Based Service Organizations
- Locating community-based service organizations: www.211.org or dial 211 on phone, www.hirenetwork.org and www.goodwill.org (click 'Job Seekers' or call 1-800-741-0186)

Legal Support
- American Civil Liberties Union (ACLU): National Prison Project Publications, 733 15th Street, NW, Suite 620, Washington DC 20005 Tel: 202/393-4930 www.aclu.org
- California Innocence Project: 225 Cedar Street, San Diego, CA 92101 Tel: 800/255-4252 619/239-0391 www.innocenceproject.org
- Centurion Ministries, Inc., 221 Witherspoon St., Princeton, NJ 08542-3215 Website: www.centurionministries.org
- Employment restrictions by state: www.naag.org (click 'The Attorney General')
- *Relief from the Collateral Consequences of a Criminal Conviction: State-by-State Resource Guide*: http://sentencingproject.org/PublicationDetails.aspx?PublicationID=486
- *After Prison: Roadblocks to Reentry*: www.lac.org (click 'free publications'; click 'criminal justice'; click 'after prison: roadblocks to reentry'; click 'what's the law')
- National Lawyers Guild, 132 Nassau St., Rm.# 922, New York, NY 10038 Tel: 212/679-5100 www.nig.org

- The Prisoner's Guide to Survival: PSI Publishing, Inc., 413-B 19th St., #168, Lynden, WA 98264 Tel: 800/557-8868 www.prisonerlaw.com Manual: $49.95

- Prison Law Office, General Delivery, San Quentin, CA 94964 Tel: 415/457-9144 www.prisonlaw.com

- Prison Legal News, 2400 N.W. 80th St., #148, Seattle, WA 98117-4449 Tel: 206/246-1022 www.prisonlegalnews.org

Re-Entry Assistance/Family and Personal Support

- Aid to Incarcerated Mothers, 32 Rutland St., 4th Floor, Boston, MA 02118 Tel: 617/536-0058

- The Center for Children of Incarcerated Parents (CCIP), PO box 41-286, Eagle Rock, CA 90041 Tel: 626/449-2470 www.e-ccip.org Dedicated to prevention of intergenerational crime and incarceration

- The Fortune Society, 53 West 23rd St., 8th Floor, New York, NY 10010 Tel: 212/691-7554 www.fortunesociety.org Dedicated to at-risk youth

- National Fatherhood Initiative, PO Box 126157, Harrisburg, PA 17112-6157 www.fatherhood.org Dedicated to well-being of children

- OPEN, Inc. (Offender Preparation and Education Network), PO Box 472223, Garland, TX 75047-2223 Tel: 972/271-1971 800/966-1966 www.openinc.org Free book for prisoners: *99 Days and a Get Up*

- The Graduate Group, PO Box 370351, West Hartford, CT 06137-0351 Tel: 860/233-2330 Website: www.graduategroup.com Book: *Opportunities for Newly Released Offenders*, $22.00

Jobs/Careers/Continuing Education (See also Chapter 14)

- Apprenticeships locator: www.careervoyages.gov (Click 'student.' Click 'apprenticeship.')

- Blackstone Career Institute, PO Box 899, Emmaus, PA 18049-0899 Tel: 800/826-9228 610/967-3323 www.blackstonelaw.com Offers Legal Assistant/Paralegal program

- JobCorps locator: http://jobcorps.dol.gov or call 1-800-733-5627

- Net-Temps Career Center www.net-temps.com Helps you find new job and manage career

- Biddle Publishing Company, PMB 103 13 Gurnet Road, Brunswick, ME 04011 www.biddle-audenreed.com Book: *Prisoner's Guerilla Handbook to Correspondence Programs in the United States and Canada*: $24.95 plus $6.00 priority shipping ($3.00 discount for prisoners)

- One-Stop Career Centers: www.careeronestop.org, www.servicelocator.org, and www.dol.gov

- SCORE Association, 409 3rd St., SW 6th Floor, Washington DC 20024 Tel: 800/634-0245 www.score.org SCORE – Counselors to America's Small Business; free business counseling and advice; low-cost workshops

- Vocational Rehabilitation locator: www.jan.wvu.edu/SBSES/VOCREHAB.HTM or call 1-202-245-1488

Personal Health and Nutrition

- AIDS Project Los Angeles (APLA), 3550 Wilshire Blvd., Suite 300, Los Angeles, CA 90010 Tel: 213/201-1600 www.apla.org Provides direct services

- American Civil Liberties Union National Prison Project, 733 15th St., NW, Suite 620, Washington DC 20005 Tel: 202/393-4930 www.aclu.org Free STD Booklet: *Play It Safer*

- Community Mental Health Service Locator: http://mentalhealth.samhsa.gov

- National Hepatitis C Prison Coalition (HCV Prison Support Project), PO Box 41803, Eugene, OR 97404 Tel: 541/607-5725 www.hcvinprison.org Free newsletter

- WORLD (Women Organized to Respond to Life-threatening Diseases), 414 13th St., 2nd Floor, Oakland, CA 94612 Tel: 510/986-0340 www.womenhiv.org Free newsletter www.adp.**.gov/RC/RC_sub.shtml (**Insert state abbreviation)

Selective Service Registration

- Verify registration: www.sss.gov or call 1-847-688-6888 (Selective Service System, Registration Information Office, P. O. Box 94638, Palatine, IL 60094-4638)

Social Security

- Locating Social Security Office: www.ssa.gov (click 'Find a Social Security Office')

- Social Security Card form SS-5: Call 1-800-772-1213 (show proof of ID, e.g., driver's license, passport, marriage or divorce record, or certification from prison or parole)

Student Loan Debt

- Contact U.S. Dept. of Education: call 1-800-621-3115 (Provide SS#. Dept. of Education can tell you who is holding the loan, how much you owe, and the address and phone number of the holder of the loan. Federal Perkins Loan requires that you pay a minimum of $40/month., while a direct loan usually requires a min. of $50/month.)

Support Organizations

Some local organizations, supported by funding from the U.S. Department of Health and Human Services, may be able to provide some assistance to individuals upon parole. Contact local agencies, explain the circumstances, and ask for their assistance. The staff at the agency will also be able to help you access other forms of assistance that might be available or refer you to agencies that can provide assistance.

Chapter 14

Resources for Continuing Education and Training

Email: sending and receiving messages (websites providing free email accounts)
- Gmail: www.gmail.com
- Hotmail: www.hotmail.com
- Yahoo: www.yahoo.com

Map Directions
- Google: www.maps.google.com
- Mapquest: www.mapquest.com

Planning and Paying for College
- ACT or SAT: www.actstudent.org and www.collegeboard.com
- Citizenship: www.uscis.gov
- Federal Financial Aid: www.federalstudentaid.ed.gov
- Free Application for Federal Student Aid: www.fafsa.ed.gov
- Financial Aid and College Links: www.going2college.org
- Mapping Your Future: www.mapping-your-future.org

Other Options
- AmeriCorps: www.americorps.gov and www.californiavolunteers.org
- Health Careers: www.makeitinscrubs.com
- Military Scholarships: www.todaysmilitary.com
- ScholarShare: www.scholarshare.com
- Sports Scholarships: www.ncaa.org
- Students with Disabilities: www.heath.gwu.edu
- Tax Benefits for Higher Education: www.irs.gov/pub.irs-pdf/p970.pdf
- Veterans Benefits: www.gibill.va.gov

Scholarships
- African American Scholarships: www.uncf.org
- Asian American Scholarships: www.apiasf.org
- Broke Scholar: www.brokescholar.com
- Free Scholarship Directories: www.fastweb.com, www.srnexpress.com, and www.collegeboard.com/pay
- Gates Millennium Scholarships: www.gmsp.org

- Latino Scholarships: www.latinocollegedollars.org, www.hispanicfund.org, and www.maldef.org
- Native American Scholarships: www.oiep.bia.edu, www.aises.org/highered/scholarships, and www.collegefund.org
- Scholarship Fraud: www.ftc.gov/scholarshipscams

Searching the Internet
- Google: www.google.com
- Yahoo: www.yahoo.com
- MSN: www.msn.com

Smart Borrowing
- EdFund: www.edfund.org and www.edwise.org

Smart Money Tips
- Identity Theft: www.ftc.gov/idtheft and www.idtheftenter.org
- Job Trends: www.bls.gov/emp
- Student Debt Help: www.studentdebthelp.org

Harvard and Stanford Universities
- Free tuition to most undergraduates from families earning less than $100,000 a year and free room and board to students from lower and middle-income families earning less than $60,000 who meet certain guidelines. Applicants must also meet academic standards.

Chapter 15

10 Things You Need to Know to Live on the Streets

FOR MILLIONS OF Americans, the housing crisis began well before it was on the front pages of newspapers. Bigotry and criminalization by an unjust system of policing and incarceration, combined with economic privation, have kept even the meager privilege of a sub-prime mortgage or slumlord lease out of reach for many. As the crisis unfolds, the number of homeless will grow.

Picture the Homeless (www.picturethehomeless.org), a social justice organization founded and led by homeless people in New York City, has joined *The Nation* to come up with a list of things you need to know to live on the street – and ways we can all build movements to challenge the stigma of homelessness and put forward an alternative vision of community.

1. **Be prepared to be blamed for your circumstances,** no matter how much they may be beyond your control. Think of ways to disabuse the public of common misconceptions. Don't internalize cruelty or condescension. Let go of your pride, but hold on to your dignity.

2. **Learn to travel light.** There is no private space to which you may retreat. You are on display 24/7. Store valuables in a safe place, only carrying around what you really need: ID and documents for accessing services, a pen, etc. You can check free email (hotmail.com, Inbox.com, Gawab.com, Yahoo! Mail, GMX mail, AIM mail) and read at the library. You can get a post office box for a fee or use general delivery (free).

3. **Learn the best bathroom options,** where you won't be rushed, turned away, or harassed. Find restrooms where it's clean enough to put your stuff down, the stalls are big enough to change in, and there's hot water so you can wash up.

4. **Learn soup kitchen schedules and menus.** Since it's difficult to have much control over when, where, and what you eat, carry with you nuts, peanut butter, or other foods high in protein. Maintain a list of soup kitchens by city and state.

5. **Food and clothing are easier to find than a safe place to sleep.** The first truth of homelessness is sleep deprivation. Always have a blanket. Whenever possible, sleep in groups with staggered schedules, so you can look out for one another, prioritizing children's needs over those of adults.

6. **Know your rights!** Knowing constitutional amendments, legal precedents, and human rights provisions can help you, even if they're routinely violated. Some cities strictly forbid selective enforcement of the law against the homeless. The

Malcolm X Grassroots Movement (http://mxgm.org) offers another resource, and the American Civil Liberties Union (www.aclu.org) has cards, brochures, fact sheets, and films.

7. **Learn about police patterns and practices.** Be polite and calm to cops, even when they don't give the same respect. Support initiatives demanding independent police accountability. Link with groups from overlapping populations of non-homeless and homeless people (i.e., black, Latino, LGBT groups) that are fighting police brutality and building non-police safety projects. Organize your own CopWatch and photograph, videotape, and publicize instances of police abuse. Consider and support models like the Los Angeles Community Action Network (www.cangress.org).

8. **The First Amendment protects your right to solicit aid (panhandling),** especially if your pitch or sign is a statement rather than a request. To succeed, be creative, funny, engaging ("I didn't get a bailout!"). Find good, high-traffic spots where the police won't bother you.

9. **Housing is a human right!** Squat. Forge coalitions with non-homeless but potentially displaced people in this era of mass foreclosures. Support the Coalition on Homelessness (www.cohsf.org), in San Francisco. Learn about campaigns against homelessness in other nations, including the Landless Workers' Movement in Brazil and the Anti-Eviction Campaign in South Africa.

10. **Don't go it alone!** Be always part of an informal network of trust and mutual aid. Start your own organization, with homeless people themselves shaping the fight for a better life and world.

Note: The United Way of America established an easy-to-remember telephone number to connect you to health and social services in your local community. The ever-expanding hotline currently serves almost 250 million Americans and is available in 46 states plus Washington, D.C., and Puerto Rico. Specially trained personnel help you, the caller, determine what services you need – for example, food banks and shelters, job training, and affordable housing options, among other supports – and provide you with relevant information on where to find those services. Visit www.liveunited.org/211 or dial 2-1-1.

Chapter 16

Toll-Free Telephone Numbers

If any of the toll-free telephone numbers belowchange, call 1-800-555-1212 for the current number.

Organization	Number
AA/NA/Support Groups Dial '0' for phone number, group/volunteer name	
Adoption/Foster Care Referral	800-543-7487
AIDS/HIV Hotline (California)	800-367-2437
AIDS/HIV Hotline (national) English 24-hour	800-342-2437
AIDS/HIV Hotline (national) Spanish 24-hour	800-344-7432
Alcohol/Drug Abuse Hotline	800-821-4357
Alcohol/Drug Programs Info and Referral	800-879-2772
Amber Foundation for Missing Children (24-hour)	800-541-0777
Attorney Complaint Hotline	800-843-9053
Attorney General, California	800-952-5225
Auto Repair Problems	800-952-5626
Baby Cal	800-222-9999
Banking Customer Complaint	800-622-0620
BIA Child Abuse Hotline	800-633-5155
Blind/Dyslexic, Textbooks on Tape	800-732-8398
Braille/Talking Book Library	800-952-5666
California Rural Legal Assistance	800-553-4503
California Smokers' Helpline (voice)	800-766-2888
California Smokers' Helpline (TDD)	800-933-4833
California Social Services	800-952-5253
California Vision Project ($20 co-pay for prescription glasses	800-766-4466)
CAL-VET Housing Info	800-952-5626
CA Self-help Center	800-222-5465
Cancer Info Service	800-422-6237
Cancer Care Inc.	800-813-4673
Child Abuse Hotline, (national)	800-799-7233
Child Abuse Hotline (California)	800-244-5373
Cocaine Hotline,	800-262-2463
Conservation Corps, California	800-952-5627

Consumer Affairs, California 800-952-5210
Consumer Credit Counseling Service 800-736-2227
Consumer Product Safety 800-638-2772
Contractor's Bond 800-834-2663
Council for Blind 800-221-6359
Crisis Hotline (national) 800-784-2433
Dental Assistance, Seniors 800-262-1213
Developmental Disabilities 800-952-5746
Doctors, Board Certified 800-776-2378
Domestic Violence Hotline (English 24-hour) 800-799-7233
Domestic Violence Hotline (TDD) 800-787-3224
D.U.I. Defense League 800-899-9394
Education Dept., GED Info 800-331-6316
Eldercare Locator 800-677-1116
EDD, Unemployment Claims 800-300-5616
Employment Discrimination 800-884-1684
Energy Assistance Line 800-433-4327
Equal Employment Opportunity Comm. 510-637-3230
Equifax Credit Info 800-685-1111
Experian Credit Info 888-397-3742
Facts of Life Info Line 800-711-9848
Fair Housing Hotline 800-468-7464
Families First 800-495-9559
Family Service America 800-221-2681
Federal Trade Commission 877-382-4357
Food Purchase, SHARE N. California 800-499-2506
Food Stamps, CA State Office 800-952-5253
Fraud/Injury, Attorney General 800-952-5225
Green Card Replacement (I-90; FD258) 800-870-3676
Habitat for Humanity (Housing) 800-334-3308
Handicapped, Commun. Asst 800-242-1565
Handicapped Crisis Line (24-hour) 800-426-4263
Health Planning 800-952-5270
Health Ins. Counsel. and Advocacy Prog. (HICAP) 800-434-0222
Healthy Families (MediCal for Children) 888-747-1222
Hearing Aid Hotline 800-521-5247
Hepatitis Foundation International 800-891-0707
HEW, 2nd Opinion on Surgery 800-331-1800
HIV Medical Assistance/Info 800-448-0440
Hospice Link 800-331-1620

Housing Discrimination 800-233-3212
Housing Urban Dev. (HUD) 800-669-9777
Identification Theft Hotline 877-438-4338
Immigrant Job Discrimination 800-255-7688
Immigration and Naturalization Service 800-375-5283
Immunization Info Hotline (English) 800-232-2522
Immunization Info Hotline (Spanish) 800-232-0233
Indian Legal Services 510-835-0284
Job Corps Hotline 877-388-8731
La Leche League International 800-525-3243
Medical Board Complaints 800-633-2322
MediCal Hotline 800-952-5253
Medicare Info and Referral 800-841-1602
Medicare Hotline (TDD) 800-325-0778
Mental Health Association 800-969-6642
Missing and Exploited Children Hotline 800-843-5678
Mobile Home Problems, CA 800-952-5276
Multiple Sclerosis Foundation 800-441-7055
NAACP Legal Defense and Educ. Fund 800-221-7822
National Consumers League 800-876-7060
National Flood Ins. Hotline 800-424-3872
Native American Service Network 800-446-3426
NCI Cancer Information 800-422-6237
Nehemiah Prog. Hous. Dev. Corp. 916-444-0789
Parents Anonymous 800-352-0336
People's Survival Guide (L.A.) 800-339-6993
People's Survival Guide (L.A.) 213-913-7333
People's Survival Guide (N. Calif.) 916-446-7904
Planned Parenthood 800-230-7526
PMS Access 800-222-4767
Poison Control (24-hour) 800-876-4766
Poison Control (24-hour) (TDD) 800-972-3323
Prisoners' Rights Union 916-441-4214
Rape, Abuse, Incest Network 800-656-4673
Rehabilitation, California 800-952-5544
Runaway Children's Center 800-621-4000
Runaway Children's Center (TDD) 800-621-0394
Safe Sitter 800-255-4089
Savings and Loan Consumer Educ. 800-792-9630
Sickle Cell Disease 800-421-8453

Self-employed Medical Plan..800-655-5544
Sibling Location..800-742-5464
Small Business Hotline...800-827-5722
Social Service Complaints, Calif. 800-952-5253
Social Security, Eligibility Info 800-772-1213
Social Security, Eligibility Info (TDD) 800-325-0778
State Insurance Hotline..800-927-4357
STD Hotline 800-227-8922
Suicide Hotline (24-hour) (voice) 800-784-2433
Suicide Hotline (TDD)..800-448-1833
Taxes. IRS, Federal Forms only 800-242-4585
Taxes, Info on Federal Taxes..800-424-1040
Taxes, Info on Calif. Taxes 800-852-5711
Taxes, Calif. (TDD)...800-622-6268
Trans Union Credit Info..800-888-4213
Venereal Diseases Hotline 800-952-5833
Veterans Affairs..800-952-5626
Veterans Affairs Benefits Info..800-827-1000
Victim of Crime Rights...800-842-8467/394-2255
Welfare...800-952-5626
WIA (formerly PIC) 800-367-2562
WIC (Women, Infants, Children Nutrition
    Program/Health Care Line 888-942-9675
Women and Children First 714-663-2446
Women and Family Crisis Asst...909-623-9751
Women Escaping Violent Environment (24-hour).......................888-303-4500
Women's Health Hotline...800-376-4636
Women's Information Line...800-221-4945
YMCA...800-872-9622
Youth Crisis Line 800-843-5200
YWCA 877-398-8143

Index

The Author

Dr. Harvey Shrum, Ed.D., has over 30 years of professional experience in re-entry, correctional education, college, secondary, and special education. He has been responsible for creating and implementing successful evidence-based life skills and re-entry programs through the Department of Corrections in California. He also has delivered training and conducted individual and group therapy relating to parenting skills, anger management, additions, and depression.

Dr. Shrum's advances in the field of re-entry are empirically proven to reduce recidivism. His published research, *"No Longer Theory: Correctional Education That Works"* (www.intensivejournal.org/specialized/article_shrum.php), has been cited in thousands of research publications for documenting two cost-effective prevention and rehabilitation programs and approaches to recidivism that really work – *Logotherapy and the Intensive Journal.*

Dr. Shrum was encouraged in his life's work by his mentor, the eminent psychologist and Holocaust survivor, Dr. Joseph Fabry. Dr. Shrum's book *Search for Meaning at the Broken Places* (Wyndam Hall, 2011) is fast becoming required reading for students of psychology and all survivors of life.

A motivational speaker, researcher, statistician, re-entry program developer, and consultant, Dr. Shrum is a frequent speaker at local, national, and international conferences as well as appears on radio and television. He can be contacted at doc@logo mentor.com.

Re-Entry Success Resources

THE FOLLOWING resources are available directly from Impact Publications. Full descriptions of each title – as well as downloadable catalogs, DVDs, software, games, posters, and related products – can be found at www.impactpublications.com. Complete this form or list the titles, include shipping (see the formula at the end), enclose payment, and send your order to:

IMPACT PUBLICATIONS
9104 Manassas Drive, Suite N
Manassas Park, VA 20111-5211 USA
1-800-361-1055 (orders only)
Tel. 703-361-7300 or Fax 703-335-9486
Email address: query@impactpublications.com
Quick & easy online ordering: www.impactpublications.com

Orders from individuals must be prepaid by check, money order, or major credit card. We accept telephone, fax, and email orders.

Qty.	Titles	Price	TOTAL
Featured Titles			
_____	The Ex-Offender's Guide to a Responsible Life	$15.95	_____
_____	Man's Search for Meaning	14.00	_____
Ex-Offenders and Re-Entry Success Books			
_____	9 to 5 Beats Ten to Life	20.00	_____
_____	The 99 Days to Re-Entry Success Journal	4.95	_____
_____	99 Days and a Get Up	9.95	_____
_____	Best Jobs for Ex-Offenders	9.95	_____
_____	Best Resumes and Letters for Ex-Offenders	19.95	_____
_____	Ex-Offender's 30/30 Job Solution	9.95	_____
_____	Ex-Offender's Job Hunting Guide	17.95	_____
_____	Ex-Offender's Job Interview Guide	9.95	_____
_____	Ex-Offender's Quick Job Hunting Guide	9.95	_____
_____	Ex-Offender Recovery and Re-Entry Success Guides	33.95	_____
_____	Ex-Offender's Re-Entry Success Guide	9.95	_____
_____	How to Do Good After Prison	19.95	_____
_____	I Need a J-O-B! The Ex-Offender's Job Search Manual	17.00	_____
_____	Life Without a Crutch	7.95	_____
_____	Man, I Need a Job	7.95	_____
_____	Putting the Bars Behind You Re-Entry Package	99.95	_____
_____	Putting the Bars Behind You Survival Guides	69.95	_____
_____	Quick Job Search for Ex-Offenders	7.95	_____
_____	Re-Entry Employment and Life Skills Pocket Guide	2.95	_____
_____	The Re-Entry Personal Finance Pocket Guide	2.95	_____
_____	Slaying the Dragon	14.95	_____
_____	Unemployed, But Moving On!	13.95	_____
Ex-Offenders Re-Entry Curriculum Program			
_____	From the Inside Out Curriculum	595.00	_____
_____	Hazelden Community Corrections Program	400.00	_____
_____	Houses of Healing Educational and Training Series	1,149.00	_____
_____	Interview Skills Survival Training Program	399.95	_____
_____	Living Skills Complete Program	1,170.00	_____

Qty.	Titles	Price	TOTAL
_____	New Direction for Ex-Offenders: A Cognitive-Behavioral Curriculum	$4,695.00	_____
_____	Psychology of Incarceration Curriculum Program	995.00	_____
_____	Ultimate Re-Entry Success Curriculum Starter Kit	1,495.00	_____

Ex-Offenders Re-Entry DVDs

Qty.	Titles	Price	TOTAL
_____	9 to 5 Beats Ten to Life	95.00	_____
_____	After Prison	129.00	_____
_____	Assignment: Re-Entry	250.00	_____
_____	Back in the World DVD Series	330.00	_____
_____	Breaking and Entering...Into a Better Life	199.95	_____
_____	Countdown to Freedom (men)	695.00	_____
_____	Countdown to Freedom (women)	695.00	_____
_____	Down But Not Out	149.00	_____
_____	Ex-Offender's Guide to Job Fair Success	129.00	_____
_____	Expert Job Search Strategies for the Ex-Offender	399.00	_____
_____	Finding a Job When Your Past Is Not So Hot	125.00	_____
_____	From Parole to Payroll	299.85	_____
_____	From Prison to Home	169.95	_____
_____	From Prison to Paycheck DVDs	999.00	_____
_____	Goin' Home: The Series	995.00	_____
_____	Housing First: Pathways Model to End Homelessness	265.00	_____
_____	How You Got Here: Reflections on a Lost Childhood	250.00	_____
_____	In Their Own Words	229.00	_____
_____	Living Free	149.00	_____
_____	Making the Right Choices: Successful Re-Entry Strategies	250.00	_____
_____	Out for Good	95.00	_____
_____	Overcoming Early Life Trauma: Creating a Second Chance	250.00	_____
_____	Parole: Getting Out and Staying Out	69.95	_____
_____	Power Source DVD Series	289.00	_____
_____	Putting the Bars Behind You	99.00	_____
_____	Re-Entry Trap: Strategies for Successful Re-Entry	250.00	_____
_____	Starting Fresh With a Troubled Background	299.95	_____
_____	Tough Questions, Straight Answers	95.00	_____
_____	The Turning Point	150.00	_____
_____	Youth Corrections DVD Series (men)	695.00	_____
_____	Youth Corrections DVD Series (women)	695.00	_____

From Addiction to Recovery

Qty.	Titles	Price	TOTAL
_____	Addiction, Recovery, and Relapse DVD Series	879.00	_____
_____	Adults and Co-Occurring Disorders DVD	225.00	_____
_____	Alcoholics Anonymous – The Big Book	16.95	_____
_____	Beat the Street: Clean and Sober in the City	750.00	_____
_____	Complete Relapse Prevention Skills Program	1,895.00	_____
_____	Drug and Alcohol Prevention DVD Series for Teens	1,095.00	_____
_____	Drugs of Addiction DVD Series	995.00	_____
_____	Living in Balance: Moving From a Life of Addiction to a Life of Recovery	549.00	_____
	Relapse Prevention Skills	99.00	_____
_____	Top 10 DVDs for Addiction and Recovery	2,095.00	_____

Qty.	Titles	Price	TOTAL
Anger and Rage			
_____	Managing Teen Anger and Violence	$19.95	_____
_____	Anger DVD	200.00	_____
_____	Anger and Conflict in the Workplace	15.95	_____
_____	Anger Control Workbook	21.95	_____
_____	Anger-Free	12.95	_____
_____	Anger Management Sourcebook	18.95	_____
_____	Angry All the Time	16.95	_____
_____	Angry Men	14.95	_____
_____	Angry Women	14.95	_____
Beyond Anger: Connecting With Self and Others DVD			
_____	Beyond Anger: A Guide for Men	14.95	_____
_____	Cage Your Rage DVD Program	495.00	_____
_____	Cage Your Rage for Teens Workbook	15.00	_____
_____	Cage Your Rage Workbook	20.00	_____
_____	Forgiveness	13.95	_____
_____	Handling Anger and Frustration DVD	99.95	_____
_____	Letting Go of Anger	16.95	_____
_____	Living With a Narcissistic and Entitled Generation Kit	309.95	_____
_____	Manhood and Violence: Fatal Peril DVD	149.95	_____
_____	Niagara Falls Metaphor: Anger, Drugs, and Relapse DVD	69.95	_____
_____	Pathways to Peace Anger Management Workbook	29.95	_____
_____	Pulling Punches: A Curriculum for Rage Management	495.00	_____
_____	Rage	16.95	_____
_____	Stop the Anger Now	21.95	_____
_____	Transforming Anger	15.95	_____
_____	Violent No More	17.95	_____
_____	You Can't Say That to Me!	18.95	_____
Family and Parenting Skills			
_____	Fathering: What It Means to Be a Dad	79.95	_____
_____	The Five Essentials of Successful Parenting DVD	199.95	_____
_____	How to Be a Responsible Father: A Workbook for Offenders	30.00	_____
_____	How to Be a Responsible Father: Instructor's Manual	50.00	_____
_____	How to Be a Responsible Mother: A Workbook for Offenders	30.00	_____
_____	How to Be a Responsible Mother: Instructor's Manual	50.00	_____
_____	Post-Prison Blues DVD	129.00	_____
_____	The Story of Fathers and Sons DVD	149.00	_____
_____	The Story of Mothers and Daughters DVD	149.00	_____
Career Exploration and Job Strategies			
_____	12 Steps to a New Career	16.99	_____
_____	40 Best Fields for Your Career	16.95	_____
_____	50 Best Jobs for Your Personality	17.95	_____
_____	95 Mistakes Job Seekers Make and How to Avoid Them	13.95	_____
_____	100 Fastest Growing Careers	17.95	_____
_____	101 Best Ways to Land a Job in Troubled Times	14.95	_____
_____	150 Best Jobs for a Secure Future	17.95	_____
_____	200 Best Jobs Through Apprenticeships	24.95	_____
_____	250 Best Paying Jobs	17.95	_____

Qty.	Titles	Price	TOTAL
_____	300 Best Jobs Without a Four-Year Degree	$17.95	_____
_____	America's Top Jobs for People Re-Entering the Workforce	19.95	_____
_____	Best Jobs for the 21st Century	19.95	_____
_____	Career Mapping	17.95	_____
_____	Change Your Job, Change Your Life	21.95	_____
_____	Cracking the New Job Market	17.95	_____
_____	Get the Career You Want	15.00	_____
_____	Get Hired in a Tough Job Market	16.95	_____
_____	Get the Job You Want, Even When No One's Hiring	19.95	_____
_____	Guerrilla Marketing for Job Hunters 3.0	21.95	_____
_____	How to Get a Job and Keep It	16.95	_____
_____	Job Hunting Tips for People With Hot and Not-So-Hot Backgrounds	17.95	_____
_____	Job Hunter's Survival Guide	9.99	_____
_____	Knock 'em Dead	14.95	_____
_____	No One Is Unemployable	29.95	_____
_____	No One Will Hire Me	15.95	_____
_____	Occupational Outlook Handbook (annual)	19.95	_____
_____	Overnight Career Choice	9.95	_____
_____	The Quick 30/30 Job Solution	14.95	_____
_____	Smart New Way to Get Hired	14.95	_____
_____	Top 100 Careers Without a Four-Year Degree	18.95	_____
_____	Top 300 Careers	18.95	_____
_____	What Color Is Your Parachute?	18.99	_____

Internet Job Search

Qty.	Titles	Price	TOTAL
_____	America's Top Internet Job Sites	19.95	_____
_____	Guide to Internet Job Searching	16.95	_____
_____	Job Seeker's Online Goldmine	13.95	_____
_____	What Color Is Your Parachute? Guide to Job-Hunting Online	12.99	_____

Interviews

Qty.	Titles	Price	TOTAL
_____	101 Dynamite Questions to Ask At Your Job Interview	13.95	_____
_____	101 Great Answers to the Toughest Interview Questions	12.99	_____
_____	301 Best Questions to Ask On Your Interview	14.95	_____
_____	301 Smart Answers to Tough Interview Questions	12.95	_____
_____	Best Answers to 201 Most Frequently Asked Interview Questions	14.95	_____
_____	Can I Wear My Nose Ring to the Interview?	13.95	_____
_____	Everything Practice Interview Book	14.95	_____
_____	I Can't Believe They Asked Me That	17.95	_____
_____	Interview Magic	18.95	_____
_____	Job Interview Tips for People With Not-So-Hot Backgrounds	14.95	_____
_____	Job Interview Phrase Book	10.95	_____
_____	Job Interviews for Dummies	16.99	_____
_____	KeyWords to Nail the Job Interview	17.95	_____
_____	Nail the Job Interview	14.95	_____
_____	The Savvy Interviewer	10.95	_____
_____	Tell Me About Yourself	14.95	_____

Qty.	Titles	Price	TOTAL
_____	Win the Interview, Win the Job	$15.95	_____
_____	You Should Hire Me	15.95	_____

Social Media

_____	Find a Job Through Social Networking	14.95	_____
_____	How to Find a Job on LindedIn, Facebook, Twitter, MySpace, and Other Social Networks	18.95	_____
_____	Twitter Job Search Guide	14.95	_____
_____	Web 2.0 Job Finder	15.99	_____

Salary Negotiations

_____	101 Salary Secrets	12.95	_____
_____	Give Me More Money	17.95	_____
_____	Salary Negotiation Tips for Professionals	16.95	_____
_____	Secrets of Power Salary Negotiating	13.99	_____

Attitude and Motivation

_____	100 Ways to Motivate Yourself	14.99	_____
_____	Attitude Is Everything	16.99	_____
_____	Change Your Thinking, Change Your Life	19.95	_____
_____	Goals	18.95	_____

Inspiration and Empowerment

_____	The 3 Essentials: All You Need for Success in Life	19.95	_____
_____	7 Habits of Highly Effective People	15.95	_____
_____	10 Dumbest Mistakes Smart People Make and How to Avoid Them	13.99	_____
_____	12 Bad Habits That Hold Good People Back	15.95	_____
_____	17 Lies That Are Holding You Back and the Truth That Will Set You Free	17.99	_____
_____	101 Secrets of Highly Effective Speakers	15.95	_____
_____	Awaken the Giant Within	16.95	_____
_____	Change Your Thinking, Change Y our Life	19.95	_____
_____	Create Your Own Future	19.95	_____
_____	Finding Your Own North Star	15.00	_____
_____	Five Great Principles for Life	23.00	_____
_____	Life Strategies	13.95	_____
_____	The Magic of Thinking Big	14.95	_____
_____	Mindset: The New Psychology of Success	16.00	_____
_____	No Excuses! The Power of Self-Discipline	15.99	_____
_____	The Power of Positive Thinking	14.95	_____
_____	Power of Purpose	17.95	_____
_____	Practical Wisdom	26.95	_____
_____	Put Your Strengths to Work	15.00	_____
_____	Rebound Rules: The Art of Success 2.0	16.99	_____
_____	Success Principles	17.99	_____
_____	StrengthFinder 2.0	24.95	_____
_____	Think Big	14.99	_____
_____	We Have Meet the Enemy	26.95	_____
_____	What You Can Change...And What You Can't	14.95	_____
_____	Who Moved My Cheese?	19.95	_____
_____	Why We Make Mistakes	14.00	_____

Qty.	Titles	Price	TOTAL
_____	Willpower	$27.95	_____
_____	The Winner's Brain	15.00	_____
_____	Winner's Manual For the Game of Life	24.99	_____

Testing and Assessment

_____	Career, Aptitude, and Selections Tests	17.95	_____
_____	Career Match	15.00	_____
_____	Discover What You're Best At	14.95	_____
_____	Do What You Are	18.99	_____
_____	Employment Personality Tests Decoded	16.99	_____
_____	The Everything Career Tests Book	12.95	_____
_____	I Want to Do Something Else, But I'm Not Sure What It Is	15.95	_____
_____	Now, Discover Your Strengths	30.00	_____
_____	What Should I Do With My Life?	16.00	_____
_____	What Type Am I?	16.00	_____
_____	What's Your Type of Career?	21.95	_____

Resumes and Letters

_____	101 Great Tips for a Dynamite Resume	13.95	_____
_____	201 Dynamite Job Search Letters	19.95	_____
_____	Best KeyWords for Resumes, Cover Letters, & Interviews	17.95	_____
_____	Best Resumes for People Without a Four-Year Degree	19.95	_____
_____	Blue-Collar Resume and Job Hunting Guide	15.95	_____
_____	Competency-Based Resumes	13.99	_____
_____	Cover Letter Magic	18.95	_____
_____	Cover Letters for Dummies	16.99	_____
_____	Cover Letters That Knock 'Em Dead	12.95	_____
_____	Create Your Digital Portfolio	19.95	_____
_____	Expert Resumes for Baby Boomers	16.95	_____
_____	Expert Resumes for Career Changers	16.95	_____
_____	Expert Resumes for Computer and Web Jobs	16.95	_____
_____	Expert Resumes for People Returning to Work	16.95	_____
_____	High Impact Resumes and Letters	19.95	_____
_____	Nail the Cover Letter	17.95	_____
_____	Nail the Resume	17.95	_____
_____	Resume, Application, and Letter Tips for People With Hot and Not-So-Hot Backgrounds	17.95	_____
_____	Resumes for Dummies	16.99	_____
_____	Resumes That Knock 'Em Dead	12.95	_____
_____	The Savvy Resume Writer	12.95	_____
_____	Step-By-Step Resumes	19.95	_____
_____	Winning Letters That Overcome Barriers to Employment	17.95	_____

Networking

_____	Fine Art of Small Talk	16.95	_____
_____	Little Black Book of Connections	19.95	_____
_____	Masters of Networking	18.95	_____
_____	Networking for People Who Hate Networkingr	16.95	_____
_____	Never Eat Alone	24.95	_____
_____	One Phone Call Away	24.95	_____
_____	Power Networking	14.95	_____

Qty.	Titles	Price	TOTAL
_____	The Savvy Networker	13.95	_____
_____	Work the Pond	15.95	_____

Dress, Image, and Etiquette

Qty.	Titles	Price	TOTAL
_____	Business Etiquette for Dummies	21.99	_____
_____	Dressing Smart for Men	16.95	_____
_____	Dressing Smart for the New Millennium	15.95	_____
_____	Dressing Smart for Women	16.95	_____
_____	Power Etiquette	15.95	_____
_____	You've Only Got Three Seconds	15.00	_____

Government and Security Jobs

Qty.	Titles	Price	TOTAL
_____	Book of U.S. Government Jobs	27.95	_____
_____	Complete Guide to Public Employment	19.95	_____
_____	FBI Careers	19.95	_____
_____	Federal Law Enforcement Careers	19.95	_____
_____	Post Office Jobs	24.95	_____
_____	Ten Steps to a Federal Job	28.95	_____

SUBTOTAL   _____
Virginia residents add 5% sales tax

POSTAGE/HANDLING $5.00 + add%
($5 for first product and 9% of SUBTOTAL)
9% of SUBTOTAL   _____
(Include an additional 15% if shipping
outside the continental United States)   _____
TOTAL ENCLOSED   _____

SHIP TO:

Name:_____

Address: _____

_____

_____

PAYMENT METHOD:

☐ I enclose check/money order for $ _____ made payable to
   IMPACT PUBLICATIONS.

☐ Please charge $ _____ to my credit card:

☐ Visa   ☐ MasterCard   ☐ American Express   ☐ Discover

Card #_____Expiration date: ____/____

Signature_____

Ex-Offender Re-Entry Guides

Cost-effective resources from 59¢ to $9.95 each

- Used by state correctional facilities as key re-entry training resources
- Emphasize taking responsibility, changing attitudes, and making smart decisions
- Jam-packed with revealing examples, interactive tests, and insightful exercises
- Easy to read and incorporate into ongoing re-entry training programs
- Can be customized around client needs (Special Edition option)

Bestseller!

Quantity discounts on books

10-24 copies .... **20% ($7.96)**	100-249 copies .... **40% ($5.97)**
25-49 copies .... **25% ($7.46)**	250-999 copies .... **50% ($4.97)**
50-99 copies .... **30% ($6.96)**	1,000+ copies .... **60% ($3.98)**

25 copies–$186.50 50 copies–$348.00 100 copies–$597.00 500 copies–$2,485.00 1,000 copies–$3,980.00

Best Jobs for Ex-Offenders

Ron Krannich, Ph.D.

Discover the best jobs for your background.

Young and inexperienced, most ex-offenders lack knowledge about job opportunities appropriate for their red flag backgrounds. This book profiles 101 jobs (outlook, nature of work, qualifications, earnings, contacts) that are open to many ex-offenders. It also identifies various jobs closed to ex-offenders. A terrific resource for exploring jobs with a future for people with difficult backgrounds. 128 pages. 2009. ISBN 978-1-57023-284-8. **$9.95**

The Ex-Offender's Quick Job Hunting Guide

Ronald L. Krannich, Ph.D.

Lead instructional text for an innovative new re-entry program in the Ohio prison system.

"Holds the potential of becoming one of the decade's most significant books . . . a force for good in changing lives and conserving public resources." – Joyce Lain Kennedy, syndicated career columnist review of companion *The Ex-Offender's Job Hunting Guide*. Packed with practical insights, self-tests, and exercises, this book is designed to implement 10 key steps for re-entering the work world. Includes special sections on changing attitudes, community assistance, networking, completing applications, writing resumes, handling rejections, interviewing, taking responsibility, being truthful, and developing an action plan. 128 pages. 2009. ISBN 978-157023-285-5. **$9.95**

The Ex-Offender's Job Interview Guide

Caryl and Ron Krannich, Ph.D.s

Tell your story, win the job – despite red flags in your background!

This book helps ex-offenders ace the critical job interview. Covers preparing for the interview, anticipating questions, dealing with red flag questions, telling your story, closing the interview, following up, job offers, and salaries. Includes sample questions and dialogues. One of the most insightful job interview books addressing key employability issues facing ex-offenders. 128 pages. 2009. ISBN 978-1-57023-282-4. **$9.95**

The Ex-Offender's Re-Entry Success Guide

Ron and Caryl Krannich, Ph.D.s

Presents a 7-step transition plan for re-entry success.

Here's the ultimate re-entry success guide for ex-offenders. While the whole re-entry process is fraught with challenges that can lead to rejections, disappointments, and temptations, it also is a time for self-renewal and transformation. This book addresses the major psychological and practical day-to-day challenges facing ex-offenders as they re-enter the free world. Eleven hard-hitting chapters outline a clear seven-step process for re-entry success. Addresses everything from attitudes, motivation, and education to telling the truth, taking responsibility, building trust, seeking community-based assistance, and leaving a legacy. Filled with useful examples and exercises as well as a purpose-driven journal for daily action planning. 128 pages. 2009. ISBN 978-1-57023-283-1. **$9.95**

The Ex-Offender's 30/30 Job Solution
Your Lifeboat Guide to Re-Entry Success

Neil P. McNulty and Ronald L. Krannich, Ph.D.

Get a job in 30 days and within 30 miles from home.

This book outlines a powerful 30-day program for finding employment opportunities within 30 miles of any location. Filled with step-by-step advice on everything from identifying employers, writing resumes, and composing emails to leaving voicemail messages, interviewing, and follow-up over a 30-day period. 128 pages. 2009. ISBN 978-1-57023-287-3. **$9.95**

The Re-Entry Employment and Life Skills Pocket Guide

Packed with essential re-entry success information, this handy pocket guide prepares ex-offenders for transitioning to the free world. 64 pages. 2009. ISBN 978-1-57023-302-9. $2.95. **SPECIALS: Quantity discounts on 10 to 100,000 copies (range from 59¢ to $2.36 each). See page 2 for longer description and discount schedule.**

CUSTOMIZED VERSIONS: Interested in quickly developing customized editions of these books with your own cover, logo, and/or content? For more information, contact Ron at Impact Publications: ron@impactpublications.com.

SPECIAL: Purchase all 6 re-entry guides for $49.95: *Ex-Offender Re-Entry Success Action* ____

Re-Entry Journal and Pocket Guides
Budget-friendly re-entry action guides – 59¢ to $4.95 each!

The 99 Days to Re-Entry Success Journal:
Your Weekly Planning and Implementation Tool for Staying Out for Good!

 New!

Ronald L. Krannich, Ph.D.

Wow – a practical how-to guide that translates re-entry into daily **goal-oriented activities!** This user-friendly journal represents the **missing link** in most re-entry programs. It helps ex-offenders handle key stages of re-entry during their first 99 days in the free world – one start-up day followed by 14 weeks of intensive planning and implementation. Focusing on the **implementation process**, it requires users to:

- specify three realistic weekly goals
- anticipate related outcomes
- make key adjustments for the next week
- identify specific supporting activities
- evaluate weekly progress toward goals
- keep an appointment calendar

Viewing re-entry as a challenging full-time job, the book requires users to write down exactly what they plan to do each day (a daily "To Do" list) and then evaluate on a scale of 1 to 10 to what degree they accomplished their goals. They then identify what to do next to better achieve their goals. The journal also includes revealing information on documentation, contacts, appointments, financial planning, and community-based resources.

Used alone or in a group setting, this book provides an essential **structure** for keeping ex-offenders **focused on** those things they need to do for successful re-entry. Best of all, it serves as a critical **motivator** for developing **new patterns of behavior** for staying out for good! 2010. 64 pages. 5½" x 8½". ISBN 978-1-57023-318-0. **$4.95**

CONTENTS
1. Prepare for Re-Entry Success
2. DAY 1 - Commit Yourself to Success
3. Plan Your Next 14 Weeks of Activities
4. Appointment Calendar/Meeting Log
5. Community-Based Service Providers
6. Directory of Key Contacts
7. Finance Your Future
8. Budget Your Income and Expenditures
9. Personal Information/Documentation
10. Major Re-Entry Plans
11. Key Re-Entry Success Resources

Author: Ronald L. Krannich, Ph.D., is one of today's leading career and travel writers who has authored more than 90 books , including several bestsellers for ex-offenders: *The Ex-Offender's Job Hunting Guide, Best Resumes and Letters for Ex-Offenders, The Ex-Offender's Job Interview Guide, Best Jobs for Ex-Offenders,* and *The Ex-Offender's 30/30 Job Solution.*

The Re-Entry Employment and Life Skills Pocket Guide

Ronald L. Krannich, Ph.D.

Bestseller!

Presents essential personal and employability information for anyone in transition. Especially useful for ex-offenders and individuals in recovery re-entering the free world. Helps users assess skills, complete applications, write resumes, conduct job interviews, negotiate compensation, and survive, thrive, and advance on the job. Offers tips on education, training, health, attitudes, financial planning, housing, transportation, and community services. Includes a useful documentation section for compiling essential personal information. 2009. 64 pages. 3 ⁷/₈" x 4 ⁷/₈". ISBN 978-1-57023-303-6. **$2.95**

The Re-Entry Personal Finance Pocket Guide

New!

Ronald L. Krannich, Ph.D., and Trudy S. Woodring

How well prepared are newly freed individuals to make smart money decisions on their own, especially if they lack basic financial skills and are "unbanked" people? Primarily designed for ex-offenders re-entering society, this handy pocket guide is jam-packed with essential tips, checklists, examples, exercises, and recommended resources for becoming more financially savvy. It offers numerous tips on how to best:

- set goals
- get insurance
- stay out of debt
- bank and save
- buy a car
- start a business
- handle credit cards
- rent an apartment
- borrow and invest

Offers sound advice to help individuals and their families deal with important financial issues throughout their lives. 2010. 64 pages. 3 ⁷/₈" x 4 ⁷/₈". ISBN 978-157023-310-4. **$2.95**

CUSTOMIZED VERSIONS:
Interested in quickly developing customized editions of these re-entry, employment, and finance pocket guides with your own cover, logo, and/or content? For more information, contact Ron at Impact Publications: ron@impactpublications.com.

Quantity Journal discounts

10-24 copies	20% ($3.96 each)
25-49 copies	25% ($3.72 each)
50-99 copies	30% ($3.47 each)
100-449 copies	40% ($2.97 each)
500-999 copies	50% ($2.48 each)
1,000-4,999 copies	60% ($1.98 each)
100,000+ copies	80% ($.99 each)

Quantity discounts on all pocket guides

Per unit discounts/costs		Quantity costs	
10-24 copies	20% ($2.36)	10 copies	$23.60
25-49 copies	30% ($2.06)	25 copies	$51.63
50-99 copies	40% ($1.77)	50 copies	$88.50
100-499 copies	50% ($1.48)	100 copies	$147.50
500-999 copies	55% ($1.33)	500 copies	$663.75
1,000-4,999 copies	60% ($1.18)	1,000 copies	$1,180.00
100,000 copies	80% ($.59)	100,000 copies	$59,000.00

SPECIALS: Purchase all 3 books for $9.95; 10 sets of 3 books for $89.95; 100 sets of 3 books for $849.95 – *Re-Entry Journal and Pocket Guides (set of 3)*

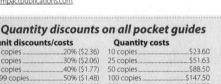